Psychology of UX Design

Psychological laws and effects | Gamification | Biases

Alok Kumar

www.bpbonline.com

First Edition 2024

Copyright © BPB Publications, India

ISBN: 978-93-65891-645

LIMITS OF LIABILITY AND DISCLAIMER OF WARRANTY

To View Complete
BPB Publications Catalogue
Scan the QR Code:

www.bpbonline.com

Dedicated to

My parents:

M.P. Gupta *and* **Prabha Kumari**

My beloved wife **Shivani** *and*

My son **Aarav**

About the Author

Alok Kumar, with two decades of industry expertise in design and innovation, serves as the Director of UX Design at Myntra, India's leading Fashion E-commerce platform. Alok brings a wealth of experience from esteemed corporations and startups, including Microsoft, Walmart, Vedantu, BlueStone, and few mobile gaming ventures.

Driven by a passion for both learning and teaching, Alok has a Masters in Psychology and is currently pursuing his Doctorate in Design while actively engaging with students at esteemed design schools such as IIT Bombay, Chitkara University, JLU Bhopal, and numerous others as a guest speaker. Through these engagements, he bridges the gap between academic learning and industry demands, ensuring students are well-prepared for real-world challenges.

Alok is also the co-founder of "RethinkingUX," a thriving UX Design community boasting over 50,000 members (UX Designers) worldwide. Committed to nurturing talent in the design realm, Alok and his team aim to empower aspiring and mid-level designers to enhance their skills and excel in the field.

At Myntra, Alok has spearheaded the development of several groundbreaking features powered by GenAI technology, including FashionGPT, Maya, and MyStylist. These innovative features showcase his dedication to leveraging Design Principles, Gamification and AI to enhance the user experience, revolutionizing the way users engage with fashion on the platform.

About the Reviewer

Satyam Tiwari is a distinguished UX and product designer, specializing in enhancing user experiences and optimizing product performance. Known for his meticulous attention to detail and user-centric approach, he excels at crafting intuitive interfaces and seamless interactions. Satyam collaborates effectively with cross-functional teams, leveraging tools like Figma, Sketch, and Adobe XD to transform innovative ideas into reality. A dedicated advocate for continuous learning, he is an avid reviewer of literature on UX, product design, and career development, sharing his insights to help professionals excel. Through his expert critiques and practical advice, Satyam empowers individuals to navigate the complexities of the tech industry and achieve their career goals. His commitment to professional growth and passion for design make him a trusted authority in the field, dedicated to fostering excellence and innovation in every project he undertakes.

Acknowledgement

I want to express my deepest gratitude to my family and friends for their unwavering support and encouragement throughout this book's writing, especially my wife, who has been my support system since the early stages of my career and has motivated me every day to share my experiences through this book.

I also want to thank an acquaintance who became my godfather 20 years ago and helped me in my initial journey. A heartfelt thank you to Mr. Narendra Singh, who is responsible for introducing me to the field of Design.

I am also grateful to BPB Publications for their guidance and expertise in bringing this book to fruition. It was a long journey of revising this book, with valuable participation and collaboration of reviewers, technical experts, and editors.

I would also like to acknowledge the valuable contributions of my colleagues and Design leaders during many years working in the Design industry, who have taught me so much and provided valuable feedback on my work.

Finally, I would like to extend my heartfelt thanks to all the readers who have shown interest in my book. Your support has been invaluable in making this book a reality. Your encouragement means the world to me.

Preface

I decided to write this book because I realized that design professionals need a solid understanding of the fundamental principles behind their design decisions, as well as a deep insight into the user's mindset. When designers comprehend how users perceive the information they present, they can effectively communicate in the user's language. This book explores the foundational laws of psychology and effects that are applicable in both design and everyday life. It delves into why users behave in certain ways due to psychological effects and biases, and how we can effectively convey information by understanding these effects and biases.

Additionally, this book explores the popular topic of gamification. There are numerous misconceptions about how to effectively incorporate gamification into projects. This book will guide you through the process of gamifying your product and help you recognize gamification mechanisms in the digital products around you. As you examine these designs, be mindful not to let cultural beliefs and prior knowledge bias your perspective. To raise your awareness, we will discuss a few biases that can impact design decisions. With this book, you will gain the knowledge and skills to become a proficient UX Designer with a deep understanding of user behavior. I hope you will find this book informative and helpful.

Section I – Psychology Laws

Psychological laws are highly valuable in design as they provide insights into human behavior, cognition, and perception, allowing designers to create more effective, user-friendly, and engaging products and experiences. Here are few psychological laws that helps the designers take impactful design decision.

Chapter 1: Fitt's Law – *It's easier to aim the bigger the target is.*

It's easier to aim the bigger the target is. Smaller the target, bigger the time to reach / interact with the target.

Chapter 2: Hick's Law – *More options lead to harder decisions*

The time and the effort it takes to make a decision, increases with the number of options. The more choices, the more time users take to make their decisions.

Chapter 3: Miller's Law – *Magic Number 7 rule*

The average person can only keep 7 (plus or minus 2) items in their working memory, more than that is always by practice.

Chapter 4: Jakob's Law – *Law of Familiarity*

It is always better to choose usual design solutions that are familiar to users. Users won't waste time learning.

Chapter 5: Tesler's Law – *Law of conservation of complexity*

If you simplify too much, you will transfer some complexity to the users. Because complexity can not be removed, it can be just transferred.

Chapter 6: Gestalt's Law – *Law of Proximity*

Proximity, similarity, continuity and a few more rules, help the brain build patterns for easy information consumption.

Chapter 7: Doherty Threshold – *The law of losing interest*

Users get disinterested after 400 ms inactivity in any process. Continuous engagement and feedback is the need of an hour.

Section II – Psychological Effects

Psychological effects play a crucial role in design by influencing how users perceive, interact with, and respond to a product or environment. Leveraging these effects can greatly enhance the effectiveness, appeal, and usability of a design. Here are few psychological effects in design that will help:

Chapter 8: Zeigarnik Effect – *The incomplete task stays in memory*

People remember incomplete tasks better than completed ones, it always hits in mind and result to make the task complete.

Chapter 9: Storytelling Effect – *Stories matters*

People remember stories better than facts alone, an impactful story stays in memory for a longer period of time.

Chapter 10: Halo Effect – *Looks change perception*

Favorable perceptions in one aspect positively impact our opinions in other areas. If one is good looking, he/she is perceived to be smart as well.

Chapter 11: Goal Gradient Effect – *Drive the motivation and speed*

As one gets closer to a goal, the inclination to reach it intensifies. People speedup when they are close to achieve their goal.

Chapter 12: Picture Superiority Effect – *Impact of a picture*

People remember pictures better than words. Pictures stays in memory for longer time and it is easy to recall.

Chapter 13: Von Restorff Effect – *Stand out to shine*

The more it stands out, more the probability to be seen. Even in a crowd if something looks big and bold, it is noticed by most of the people.

Section III – Gamification

Gamification refers to the application of game-design elements and principles in non-game contexts to enhance user engagement, motivation, and overall experience. In design, gamification leverages elements such as points, badges, leaderboards, challenges, and rewards to encourage users to interact more deeply with a product or service. Here are few gamification elements to learn and use in Designs:

Chapter 14: Gamification in UX Design – This chapter will explore several psychological principles in UX design that influence human behavior like, scarcity, where limited items or time create perceived value and urgency; social proof, where individuals align actions with those of others; reciprocation, fostering a sense of obligation to give back; reinforcement (positive and negative), leveraging rewards and consequences to motivate; and shared commitment, where trust and familiarity with others influence behavior. These principles illustrate how human decision-making is shaped by social dynamics and psychological triggers.

Section IV – Biases

Design, like many fields, is subject to various cognitive biases that can affect how designers create and users perceive and interact with products. Understanding these biases is crucial for creating more effective and user-centered designs. Here are some common biases in design:

Chapter 15: Biases in UX Design – This chapter will explore various cognitive biases that affect UX design like confirmation bias, where individuals seek evidence supporting their beliefs; negativity bias, which prioritizes negative memories; research bias, skewing outcomes to fit social norms; default bias, favoring familiar habits; and anchoring bias, where initial information heavily influences perceptions of truth and reliability.

Coloured Images

Please follow the link to download the
Coloured Images of the book:

https://rebrand.ly/v6zy7np

We have code bundles from our rich catalogue of books and videos available at **https://github.com/bpbpublications**. Check them out!

Errata

We take immense pride in our work at BPB Publications and follow best practices to ensure the accuracy of our content to provide with an indulging reading experience to our subscribers. Our readers are our mirrors, and we use their inputs to reflect and improve upon human errors, if any, that may have occurred during the publishing processes involved. To let us maintain the quality and help us reach out to any readers who might be having difficulties due to any unforeseen errors, please write to us at :

errata@bpbonline.com

Your support, suggestions and feedbacks are highly appreciated by the BPB Publications' Family.

Piracy

If you come across any illegal copies of our works in any form on the internet, we would be grateful if you would provide us with the location address or website name. Please contact us at **business@bpbonline.com** with a link to the material.

If you are interested in becoming an author

If there is a topic that you have expertise in, and you are interested in either writing or contributing to a book, please visit **www.bpbonline.com**. We have worked with thousands of developers and tech professionals, just like you, to help them share their insights with the global tech community. You can make a general application, apply for a specific hot topic that we are recruiting an author for, or submit your own idea.

Reviews

Please leave a review. Once you have read and used this book, why not leave a review on the site that you purchased it from? Potential readers can then see and use your unbiased opinion to make purchase decisions. We at BPB can understand what you think about our products, and our authors can see your feedback on their book. Thank you!

For more information about BPB, please visit **www.bpbonline.com**.

Join our book's Discord space

Join the book's Discord Workspace for Latest updates, Offers, Tech happenings around the world, New Release and Sessions with the Authors:

https://discord.bpbonline.com

Table of Contents

Section II – Psychological Effects

Section III – Gamification

Section IV – Biases

Section I
Psychology Laws

Psychological laws are highly valuable in design as they provide insights into human behavior, cognition, and perception, allowing designers to create more effective, user-friendly, and engaging products and experiences. Here are few psychological laws that helps the designers take impactful design decision.

CHAPTER 1
Fitt's Law

*"It's easier to aim when the target is bigger.
The smaller the target, bigger the time to reach / interact with the target."*

Introduction

Fitts' law is a predictive model that asserts that the time it takes for a person to move a pointer, such as a mouse cursor, to a target area depends on the ratio of the distance to the target and the size of the target. Thus, the longer the distance and the smaller the target's size, the longer it takes to reach the target, or complete a task.

Structure

This chapter will be covering the following topics:

- History
- How to avoid Fitt's law mistakes?

Objectives

Once you understand the Fitt's law fundamentals well, you will be able to decide what should be the size and distance of your target so that it is easier to complete the task in the expected time. There are a lot of technicalities around the minimum size of the target on different device and resolution. Understanding this law will empower with the skill of deciding the placement of your tappable objects in your design. Moreover, how do we make sure that the visual affordance of the target area is very positive in user's mind.

History

In 1954, psychologist *Paul Fitts*, aimed to find the bandwidth of human movement; how many repetitive movements could be performed in each time interval. He was influenced by *John Miller's* **Magic Number 7 Theory**. He did several experiments involving such repetitive movements and as a result he came up with the Fitts's Law, one of the most famous laws of human-computer interaction.

What *Fitt* discovered is that the time required to acquire a target depends on the distance to it, yet it is inversely proportional to its size. By his law, fast movements and small targets result in greater error rates. The bigger the target size, smaller the time to reach the target.

Fitts' Law is widely applied in **User Experience (UX)** and **User Interface (UI)** design. For example, this law influenced the convention of making interactive buttons large (especially on finger-operated mobile devices). Furthermore, smaller buttons are more difficult and time-consuming to click. Likewise, the distance between a user's task/attention area and the task-related button should be kept as short as possible. It also aims to keep the next action items closer to the last one so that focus and fingers do not move a lot for the next action because that will cause delay in performing the next action. If you refer to *Figure 1.1,* you will realize how the **Distance (D)** between mouse cursor and the target is dependent on the size of **Target (W)**.

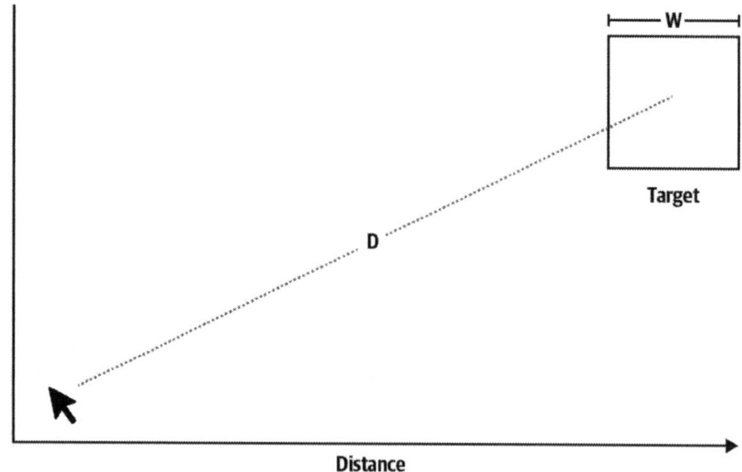

Figure 1.1*: The Distance (D) between mouse cursor and the target is dependent on the size of Target (W)*

Let us now understand Fitt's law in a simplified manner:

- The bigger the distance to the target, the longer it will take for the pointer to move to it. In other words, closer targets are faster to acquire.

- The larger the target, the shorter its movement time. In other words, bigger targets are better. Let us understand this with *Figure 1.2* below:

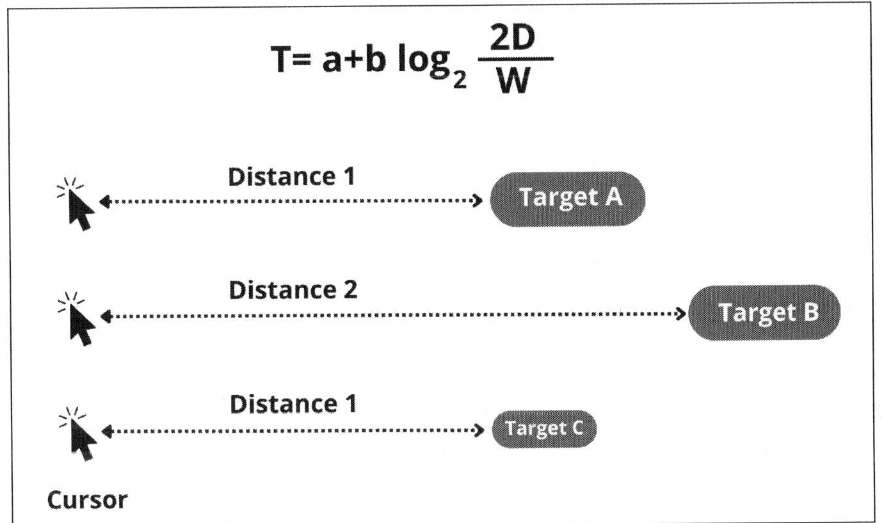

Figure 1.2: *Movement time is smaller when the target is bigger or closer*

When you refer to *Figure 1.2*, you will notice the relationship between distance and target size.

Fitts' s law says that the time to reach **Target A** is shorter than the time to reach any of the other targets. Although targets **A** and **B** have the same size, the distance from cursor to **Target A** (**Distance 1**) is shorter than the distance to **Target B** (**Distance 2**), hence, the movement to **Target A** will be faster. **Target C** is placed at the same distance (**Distance 1**) from the cursor as **Target A**, but as it is smaller, it will take longer to move the cursor to it than to **Target A**.

How to avoid Fitt's law mistakes?

It has been observed that designers often make the mistake of following Fitts's Law in their design which consequently makes the user's life a little miserable. We will now discuss how we make sure that we let the users complete their tasks as soon as possible so they reach their target within the expected time.

Bigger target sizes

Bigger the size of the target, the easier and faster it is to complete the task. Hence, there is a defined guideline for the minimum size of any actionable item in the layout, which has been explained further.

Example of iOS and material guideline for size of action buttons (minimum size):

- Human Interface Guidelines (Apple): 44 × 44 pt
- Material Design Guidelines (Google): 48 × 48 dp
- Web Content Accessibility Guidelines: 44 × 44 CSS px

If you go below these sizes, users might struggle to click / tap on the action button / icon.

Now since we are discussing icons, do you think icons are enough as an action item? here, let us remember Fitt's law: the bigger the better. Hence, to make it more convenient for the users, it is advised to have both icons + text.

This has two benefits:

- Few icons might not be self-explanatory or intuitive, so text will help the user understand before acting.
- Icon + text will take more area and the tappable/actionable area becomes bigger and as we learn - the bigger the better. It will make your user's life easier to reach to the icon + text and it will be quicker to tap / click on the action.

Figure 1.3: Icon versus Icon + text

Example of suboptimal usage of Fitt's Law

Below example has a smaller area to tap the icon plus, difficult to relate with icons, (refer to *Figure 1.4*). This is the bottom navigation of the Slice app. It looks difficult to tap because of a smaller tappable area. Moreover, these icons are not intuitive enough to tell the user what to expect before we tap on these:

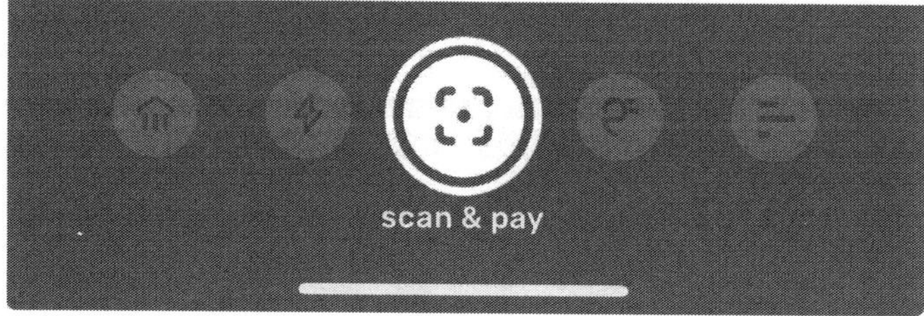

Figure 1.4: Bottom navigation of an app. It is difficult to comprehend before you tap on icons

Examples of good usage of Fitt's Law

Myntra / Coin / Swiggy have text and icon on their apps which consequently increases the size of actionable area making it easier to act on it. If you refer to the following *Figure 1.5*, you will notice how Myntra's bottom navigation is easy to tap and easy to understand as well:

Figure 1.5: *Myntra's bottom navigation panel*

Similarly, Zerodha, (refer to *Figure 1.6*) of the Coin app has an extremely comprehendible bottom navigation. They have given their users enough tapping area to select any desired option. The following text the icon makes it easier to know what to expect before we tap:

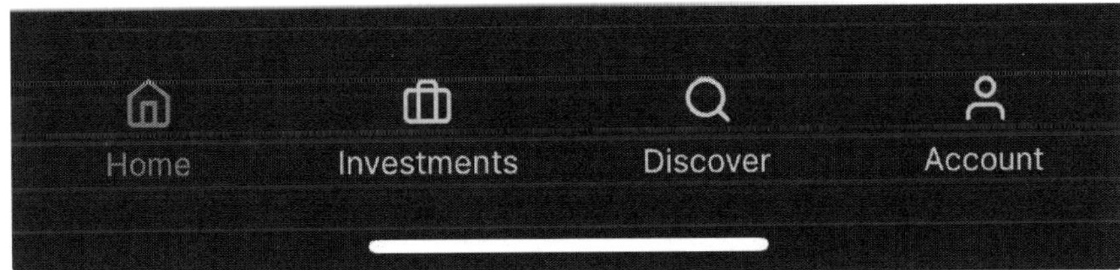

Figure 1.6: *Zerodha's bottom navigation panel*

Swiggy (refer to *Figure 1.7*) also took the same approach to showcase what they are offering, in the bottom navigation:

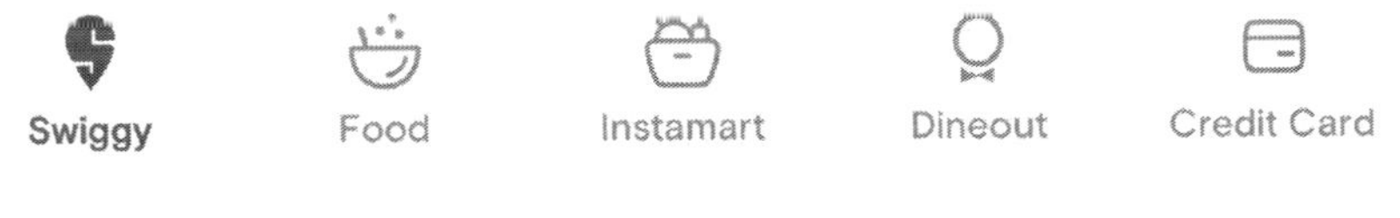

Figure 1.7: *Swiggy's bottom navigation panel*

Optimum distance between actionables

If you place targets too close to each other, there is a risk that people will accidentally overshoot and accidentally trigger the wrong target. Note that this is likely to happen if the targets are small.

Padding refers to the space between UI elements. It is an alternative spacing method to keylines and is measured in increments of 8dp or 4dp. It can be measured both vertically and horizontally and does not need to span the whole height of a layout. Refer to the following *Figure 1.8* to understand how space between two components is decided in material design (Google's Design System as shown in the following figure):

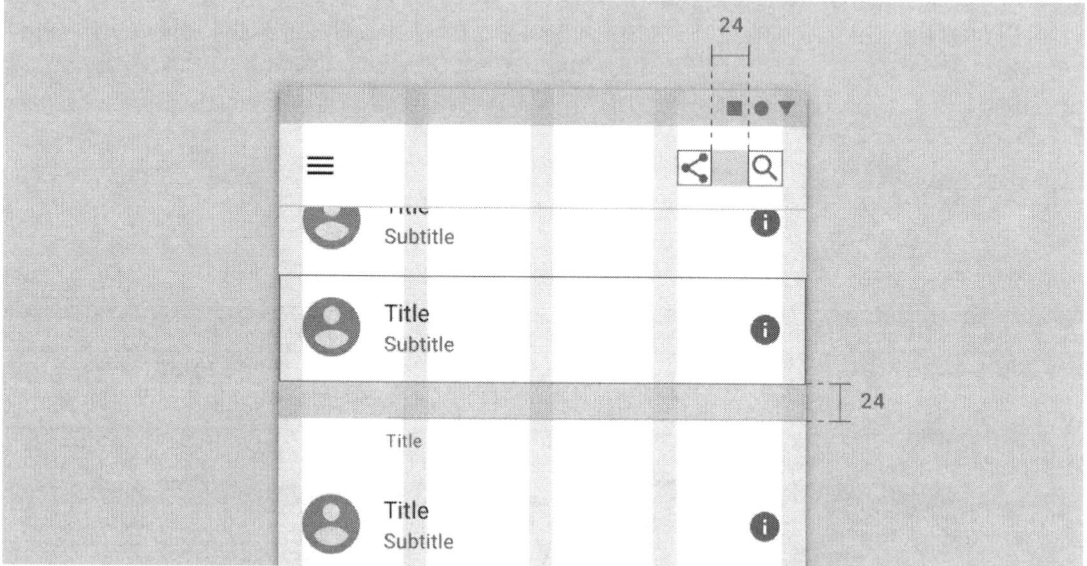

Figure 1.8: *Space between 2 components is decided in material design*
(**Source**: *https://m2.material.io/design/layout/spacing-methods.html#containers-and-ratios*)

Next action and target area need to be nearby

Think of a UI Action item on the top of your mobile screen and when you click that, an actionable list of items appears from the bottom of the screen. How convenient it is for the user to move their finger from the top of the screen to the bottom of the screen. You might also be moving from single hand to double hand or vice versa. Similarly, you are taking an action at the bottom of your mobile screen and the next action you need to take is at the top of the screen, you are going to struggle to shift your finger and focus on both, from bottom to top. This is where Fitt's law is flawed. The space between two action items is increasing and that will further increase the time of action.

For example, let us look at image editing option in iOS 16. If you observe, the editing option in iOS 16 is available at the top right of the screen as text link in blue (refer to the below *Figure 1.9*):

Figure 1.9: Image Editing option in iOS 16

In *Figure 1.9*, you will have noticed that the option to edit the image is at the top right. Once you tap on Edit, the options to edit an image appears at the bottom of the screen (see *Figure 1.10*):

Figure 1.10: Options to edit the image

Moreover, once you are done editing your image according to your requirements, you will find the option to finish at the top left of the screen. Did you notice the shift of your fingers and focus moving from top to bottom and then bottom to top? This adds extra time to complete a task. We find this experience a little sub optimal.

Let us observe another example from iOS 16, focusing on the same feature, which is the image. We should also note that to delete an image in iOS 16, (refer to *Figure 1.11*), the option is in the bottom right, as a trash icon:

Figure 1.11: *Option to delete the image*

The option to delete an image is close to my finger at the bottom right with a delete icon, since this icon is universally accepted and the size is more than 44 pt, so it is perfect in terms of visual affordance and Fitt's law rule of adequate size for action items. Now once we tap on the icons with the intent to delete the image, we get the option to delete the photo or cancel as confirmation. It is convenient to click on it faster, as it is close to the last action area, which is the delete icon, (refer to *Figure 1.12*). Hence, this reduces the time between two actions. It is a perfect example of Fitt's law:

Figure 1.12: The delete option is accessible, as it is close to the last action area

Let us talk about another very good example of keeping next action items closer to reduce the time taken to perform the action. Refer to the below *Figure 1.13* and *Figure 1.14*, which shows the Swiggy app interface:

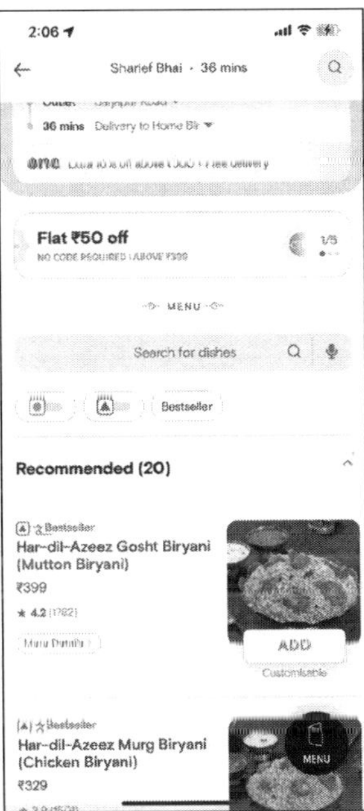

Figure 1.13: Swiggy app- FAB icon

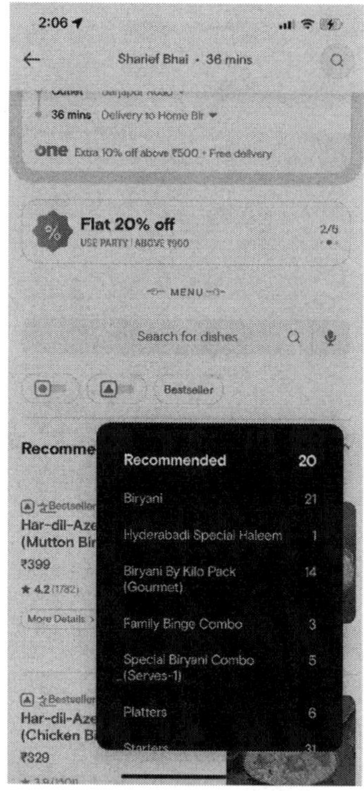

Figure 1.14: Swiggy app- FAB icon expanded

If we look through the app, we can notice a few very distinct things. Looking for food on Swiggy? Explore the recommended food and details at the top part of any restaurant page. If you want to explore the complete menu, that also comes with a handy **Floating Action Button (FAB)** which again is close to your thumb so, you can access it easily. The moment you tap on Menu, your option to take further actions appears at the same place. Which makes it easier for your finger to navigate, resulting in a shortened time between actions. Did you find this useful? This is another good example of the best use of Fitt's law.

Target at the edge of the screen

As per Fitt's law if the target is big, it is faster to reach the target area. Moreover, if the target is kept at the end/edge, it is faster to reach the goal because there is no chance of overshooting. When you aim to reach to your target quicker, you move your mouse pointer faster to reach to the edge of the screen and stop at the end or the edge of it. Let us now observe real-life examples of the same.

Have you ever observed the **Main** menu in Apple computers? It is at the top left. It is not easy to reach the main menu as soon as possible knowing that it is available at the top left of the screen. Since it is at the edge, there is no chance of overshooting when you are aiming for the option via mouse or trackpad. Refer to *Figure 1.15* and observe a MacBook desktop screen:

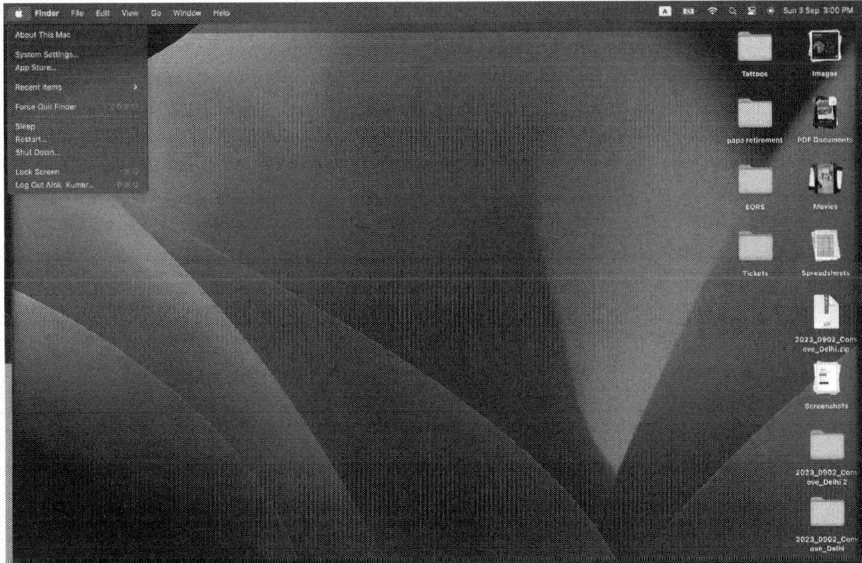

Figure 1.15: *Main menu of Apple computers (Mac OS)*

You will find similar instances in Microsoft Windows OS, and Windows 8, which have their start buttons at the bottom left edge which made it easier to reach the place we start any of the applications. Refer to *Figure 1.16*, you will observe the Windows desktop screen with the **Start** menu at the edge (bottom left):

Figure 1.16: *Windows Start menu*

Another example is that when we look at keyboards, usually the *esc* button is at the top left (refer to *Figure 1.17*). Have you ever thought of what happens when we tap the *esc* button?

Figure 1.17: ESC button on keyboards is at the top left, hence there is no chance of overshooting it or pressing another button

Let us think of this scenario: At times, when you take an action while working on a computer and make a mistake, you will want to stop it immediately. Hence to cancel your last action, you look for *esc* button. Imagine if the *esc* button could have been at the place of *M* Alphabet key/button. Would it be possible to approach it as soon as possible? You could have been struggling to figure out your *esc* button and not performed the immediate action you wanted to take. So, by placing the *esc* button at the extreme top left of the keyboard, users find it convenient to reach the *esc* button immediately.

Fitt's law is not just for digital products, hence if you observe the objects around you, you will find a lot of good and bad examples of Fitt's law. So as a UX designer, we should keep our eyes open and observe the various working examples of Fitt's law, frequently.

Conclusion

Fitt's law suggests that we keep the actionable items bigger and closer so that the time taken in performing the action is smaller. As designers we must use this law while designing digital solutions for web/mobile.

Fitts's law is one of the most useful laws of psychology that UX designers must use, but it is not foolproof, and we recommend that you do not use it blindly. Always have an eye on the data as well, and observe your user's behavior, sometimes it is possible that your users are used to a few behaviors that might not be completely right as per Fitt's law. Hence, consider tracking the way users use your website/app and optimize its design for usability and conversions. Remember, that Fitts's law should never be a hard rule in user experience design, but it should always be an essential guideline.

Overall, Fitts's law provides a valuable framework for understanding and optimizing human-computer interactions, and it continues to be relevant in fields like user experience design, ergonomics, and human-computer interaction research.

In the next chapter, we will discuss about Hick's law. It is another insightful law of psychology that impacts your design and how decision making is difficult if the number of options are more than they should be.

CHAPTER 2
Hick's Law

*"More options lead to harder decisions. The time and the effort it take to make a
decision increases with the number of options. The more choices, the more
time users take to make their decisions."*

Introduction

Hick's Law, also known as the Hick-Hyman law, is a psychological principle that describes
the relationship between the number of choices or stimuli presented to a person and the
time it takes for them to make a decision. The law suggests that increasing the number of
options or choices available to an individual will also increase the time it takes for them to
make a decision.

According to Hick's law, the time it takes for a person to make a decision increases
logarithmically with the number of choices they have. In other words, as the number of
stimuli or options increases, the decision-making process becomes more complex and
time-consuming.

In essence, Hick's law asserts that decision time is influenced by the amount of information
or alternatives a person has to consider. The more choices they have, the longer it will
typically take them to make a decision. This law is often used to emphasize the importance
of simplicity and minimalism in design, particularly in user interface design and **User
Experience (UX)** design. Designers apply this principle to reduce decision-making

complexity for users and improve the usability by presenting information or choices in a clear and organized manner.

History

Hick's Law (or the Hick-Hyman Law) is named after a British and an American psychologist team of *William Edmund Hick* and *Ray Hyman*. In 1952, this pair set out to examine the relationship between the number of stimuli present and an individual's reaction time to any given stimulus. As you would expect, the more stimuli to choose from, the longer it takes the user to make a decision on which one to interact with. The users who are bombarded with choices, have to take time to interpret and decide, giving them work they do not want.

The history of Hick's Law can be summarized as follows:

Initial research by *William Edmund Hick* in 1952 stated that Hick conducted a series of experiments to investigate the relationship between the number of stimuli or choices and the time it takes for a person to respond to a given stimulus. He used simple tasks like pressing a button in response to a light being illuminated and found out that as the number of possible choices increased, and so did the time it took for a person to decide.

In the Hick-Hyman Experiment in 1952, Hick's work was further expanded upon by *Ray Hyman* in the same year. Together, they conducted experiments that confirmed and extended Hick's findings. They demonstrated that decision time increases logarithmically with the number of choices. This means that as the number of choices doubles, the decision time also increases.

In the Law's formulation, Hick's Law was eventually formulated as a mathematical equation that describes the relationship between the number of choices (n) and the time it takes to make a decision (T):

$$T = a + b * log2(n)$$

In this equation, a and b are constants that depend on the complexity of the task and the individual's cognitive processing speed.

Regarding applications in design, Hick's Law has found significant applications in various fields, including user experience and interface design. Designers use this law to optimize the presentation of choices and reduce decision-making time for users. For example, in website design, minimizing the number of menu items or options on a page can improve user navigation and usability.

For limitations and modern interpretations, while Hick's law provides valuable insights into decision-making, it is important to note that it does not account for factors such as familiarity with the choices, individual differences, and task complexity. Modern interpretations of the law often consider these additional factors to create more accurate models of decision-making in various contexts.

Let us understand Hick's law

Let us understand Hick's law with some examples around us. There are multiple physical products in our day to day life as well as digital products where we may experience Hick's law. We will start with our TV remote. (refer to *Figure 2.1*):

Figure 2.1: *Different types / approach of TV Remote controls*

Have you ever noticed your home's TV remote which you have been in possession of for so many years? Yes, we are talking about your older TV remotes, not an Apple TV or MI TV remote (in case you have upgraded your entertainment system). There has been a conventional way of looking at TV remotes where every option is available on the remote as a button and till the time it has not become the part of your muscle memory, you must look at your remote, touch and feel the button before you tap. In case you went to a friend's home and got another TV remote, you have to spend a good amount of time understanding where your favorite action items are. It is happening because there is a lot of cognitive loads due to so many buttons and it increases the duration of the action.

At the same time if you look at Apple TV or MI TV remotes, you see very limited buttons that reduce your cognitive load, and you take action looking at your TV because it has transferred the complexity to the TV interface itself. Hence, information can be effectively organized and progressively disclosed within menus, and you have very limited buttons to interact with.

It is a great example of how to reduce cognitive load of the user for quicker decision making.

Real life examples from the UX world

Let us look at few real-life digital product examples to understand the Hick's law in detail. Refer to *Figure 2.2*, I am sure it looks similar to you:

Figure 2.2: Google homepage which is a minimalistic design

If you login to access Google, you realize that it has no extra action items other than just a search box and search call to actions. Google keeps the decisions required to enter a keyword to a minimum by eliminating any additional content that could distract from the act of typing a keyword or require additional decision-making. It keeps the user focused on the actual goal and one goal that is search. It reduces the time to think about any other action and users perform searches.

This is an interesting example of how UX designers can use Hick's law. You need to prioritize your information architecture in a manner that you have a very clear stack ranked feature list with you, helping you prioritize the most important information. We will observe another example in *Figure 2.3* now, which is an example of vast Information architecture:

My markets

Consumer Electronics >

Apparel & Accessories >

Vehicle Parts & Accessories >

Sports & Entertainment >

Industrial Machinery >

Home & Garden >

Beauty >

All categories >

Garden Supplies

Garden Gloves & Protective Gear
Pest Control
Garden Hand Tools
Watering & Irrigation
Garden Pots & Planters
Garden Buildings

Home Storage & Organization

Portable Wardrobes
Garage Shelves
Small storage & organisers
Kids & Teen Storage
Hooks & Wall Organisation
Drawers & Cabinet Organizers

Household Cleaning Tools & Accessories

Laundry Products
Cleaning Cloths
Lint Removers
Brooms & Dustpans
Cleaning Brushes
Lint Rollers & Brushes

Household Scales

Baby Scales
Body Fat Scales
Jewelry Scales
Spoon Scales
Kitchen Scales
Luggage Scales

Lighters & Smoking Accessories

Other Lighters & Smoking…
Cigarette Cases
Hookahs
Ashtrays
Cigar Cases/Humidors
Matches

Home Decor

Plaques
Clocks
Vases
Blinds, Shades & Shutters
Poufs
Decorative Flowers, Wreaths and…

Figure 2.3: *Mega Menu of one of the E-commerce Website*

Let us discuss real-life examples that UX Designers face usually. You got a long list of menu items to show. Imagine that you work for Walmart or Alibaba kind of store website that sells almost everything. And in their menu list you must show all the items. If you want to follow Hick's law and you want to remove themes from the menu list, business and product managers will not let you do so. So how are you going to help, in this scenario?

For making a big list of such type following Hick's law, you need to focus on few items.

- Items are in some order
- Items are in a group
- Items are known to users

We will look at a few examples in subsequent pages to understand in these in detail:

- **Items are in some order**: Make sure that the list you are making is in a particular order, you might figure out by arranging those alphabetically or by category. Or you might choose the right icon to connect with the option/copy mentioned. The goal here is that user's eyes should be able to scan It easily (refer to the following figure):

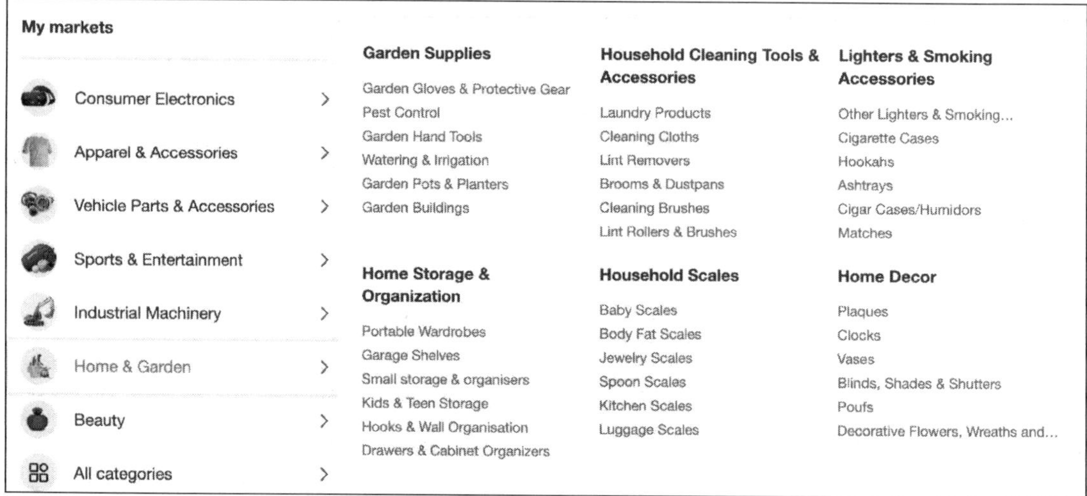

Figure 2.4: Category menu of an E-commerce website (Items in order)

- **Items are in a group**: Make sure that you group those in the right manner. It should also be a group that your users may relate to. It could be by category, by price, or by user actions. You may take this call by conducting card sorting exercises with a few of your users to understand their mental model. Refer to *Figure 2.5* to observe the items in a particular group to make it easy to scan and easy to find relevant category or group:

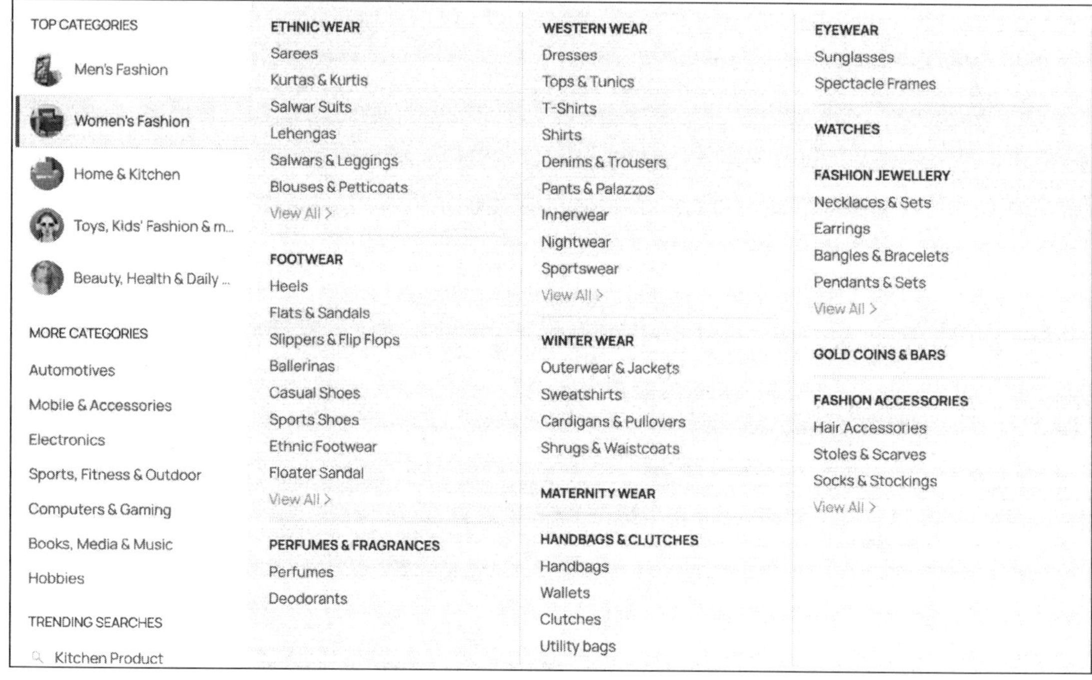

Figure 2.5: Mega menu of E-commerce website (items in group)

- **Items are known to users**: Most importantly you need to make sure that you speak the user's word. The name of the category and groups you are going to mention should be very well understood by your users. It must be very easy to understand words.

Let us look at another example of showcasing multiple options and helping users to conclude and choose an option as soon as possible.

Following are five plans with different benefits and prices and its comparison table for the users to take a final decision after comparison. Here the same Hick's law is applied. The designer took a call to highlight one of the plans which is not the cheapest, not the best, and not the most expensive but it is highlighted as the best choice. It helps the users make decisions quicker.

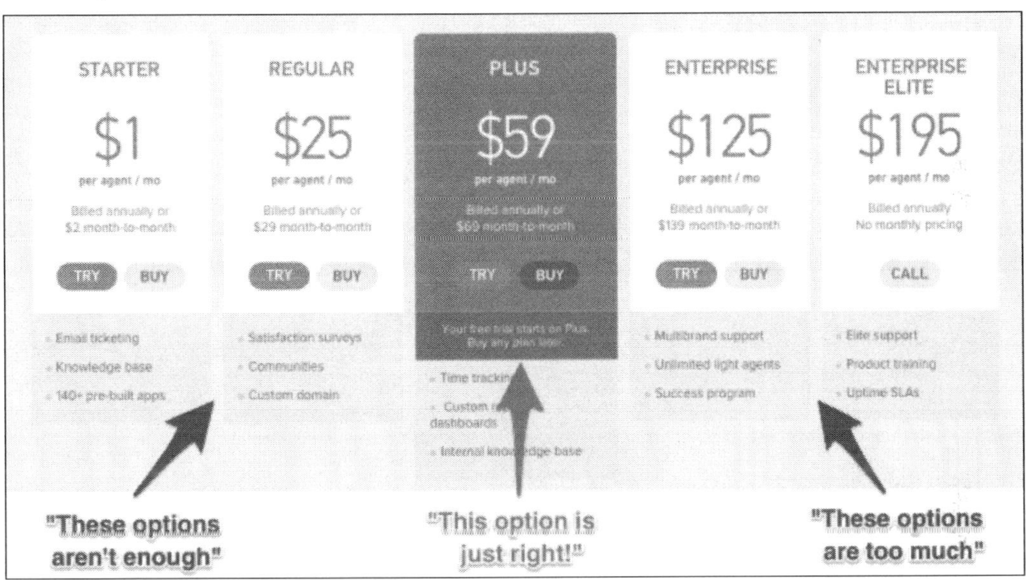

Figure 2.6: Highlighted is the best offer for users

Hence, if we look at the preceding examples (refer to *Figure 2.6*), we can say that the major functions of Hick's law are:

- To direct users to functions of top priority
- To help users reach CTA's faster
- To ensure user's do not get confused on a page

Now, to achieve the above goals/functions, it is a designer's responsibility to figure out how to make decisions quickly. It could be achieved by doing the following:

- Reducing options
- Breakdown options in steps
- Showing all the options but figuring out ways to help users make decisions quicker.

Let us understand these in detail:

Reducing options: The core idea behind Hick's Law can be condensed into a simple phrase, *simplicity equals speed*. This means that by offering only the most critical choices, you can accelerate a user's reaction time. *Figure 2.7* is from Urbanic London where you can see the minimum amount of information for a product so that it is easier for the users to take the decision quicker. For buying a top, all you need to see is the picture, know the name and its price. It is Urbanic's marketing decision of not showing lot of other information like offer, brand, color, and so on. thus, leading its website to have minimal information. This is enough for the users to take the decision faster and checkout as soon as they can. For instance, let us look at the given figure as an example:

Figure 2.7: Urbanic listing screen

Refer to another screenshot (see *Figure 2.8*) which is from Zepto (a grocery delivery app in India), if you notice they have mentioned **Add** button over their product listing page only. I am sure they believe that having an **Add** button here reduces my steps to go inside and look at more information and might get confused as well. For buying a can of *Coca Cola* or milk, all the user needs to know is the brand and quantity (in ml) and quickly add it to their cart and checkout:

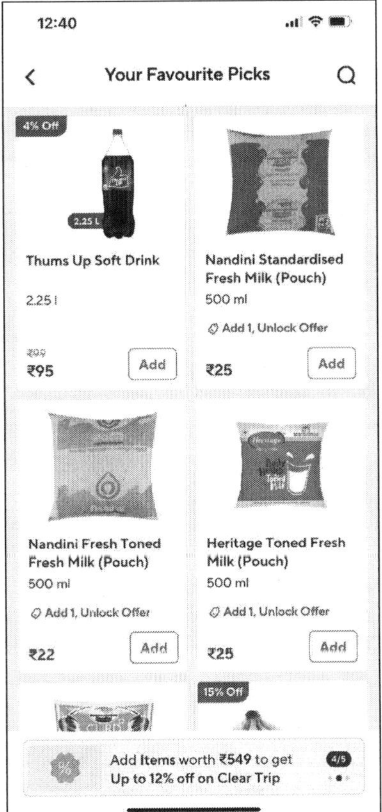

Figure 2.8: Zepto listing screen

If you notice both the above examples show how to reduce the options and reduce the information to make the decision quicker, because your user need not spend more time in decision making. This will certainly make your product conversion better. Hence, if you know the most important information, the user merely needs to take a final call.

You can also apply Hick's law to your website by dividing intricate processes, such as the checkout procedure, into more manageable stages. For instance, users can review and modify their cart on one page, input their shipping details on the subsequent page, and provide payment information on the following one. This approach to breaking down the checkout process is demonstrated by *Riot Swim*.

On the other hand, Myntra's checkout process shows information step by step, the *Figure 2.9* you can see only Cart where you need to focus on your product details and price detail of your product in your buying journey. In the following figure you may cross check the details of the products you are going to buy:

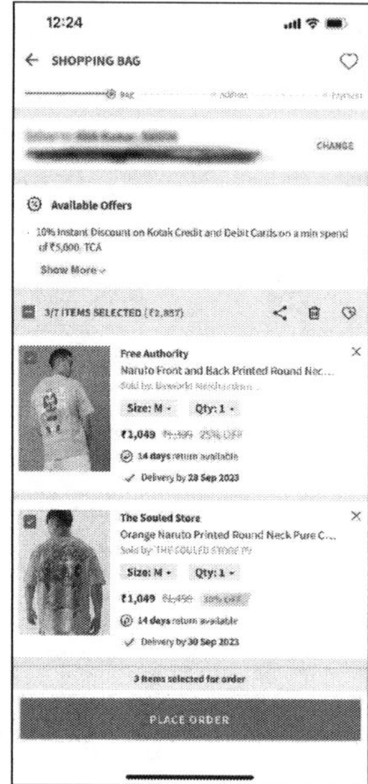

Figure 2.9: *Myntra Shopping bag*

Once you click on **Place order** in the last screen, you reach the next screen (see *Figure 2.10*), expectation is that you must have reviewed the details of the product and prices, Here, in this screen you are supposed to focus on the next steps that is selecting or adding the delivery address.

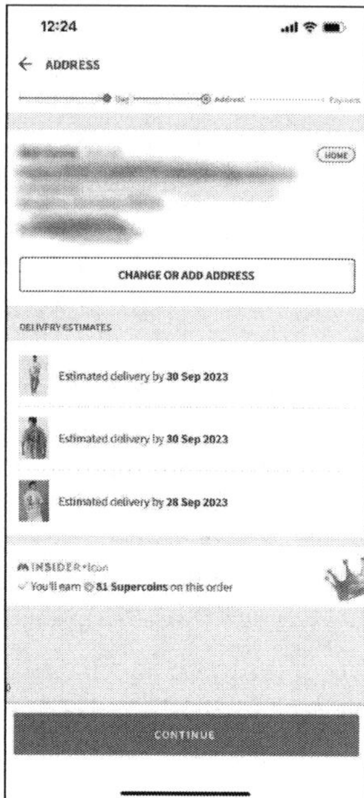

Figure 2.10: *Myntra address*

Once you have checked the product detail and price along with the desired address, it is time to make the payment as shown in *Figure 2.11*. You need to now choose your payment method to complete your transaction.

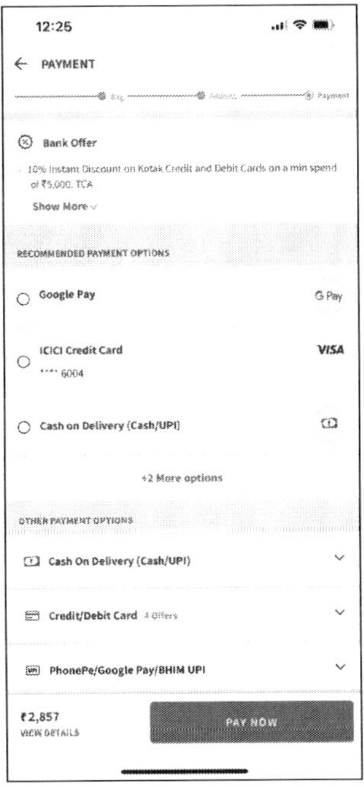

Figure 2.11: Myntra Payment screen

In this example you may notice that the e-commerce app needs all this information to deliver your product on time and at the right place for which few of the information and the payment is important, but it never put all the questions in front of you and so burdens you with a lot of need. Alternatively, it asks you questions step by step so that you are not overwhelmed with a lot of data to enter. You never realize that you must give a lot of information as well as we need to make sure that you do not miss any important information. By breaking the information step by step, it helps you to complete the process faster and it also motivates the users to easily enter the information.

Showing all the options but figuring out ways to help users make decisions quicker: To expedite a user's decision-making process, you can draw attention to or give preference to a suggested choice in your design. Take Smashing magazine's cookie consent form as an illustration. Within this form, users are presented with three choices: accepting the cookies, declining them, or exploring more about the magazine's privacy settings. The suggested option, which is to accept the cookies, stands out with the use of a distinctive color and an emoji.

Now look at the below example of Netflix subscription plan in India (refer to *Figure 2.12*). Netflix could figure out that people are watching Netflix on their mobiles a lot, so it has a specific plan to watch videos on mobile but also it has few other plans too and considering the user need and behavior. Netflix is trying to encourage the users by highlighting one of the best suited one. Mentioning all the most important information in the comparison table but also highlighting second plan which is Basics to emphasize the users to take the decision quicker. It is possible that Netflix would have experienced the Basic plan as the most selling subscription plan so rather than only putting all the information in the comparison table, Netflix highlighted one option for you so that you can compare or easily find the highlighted one the best for you and it will result in quickly decision making.

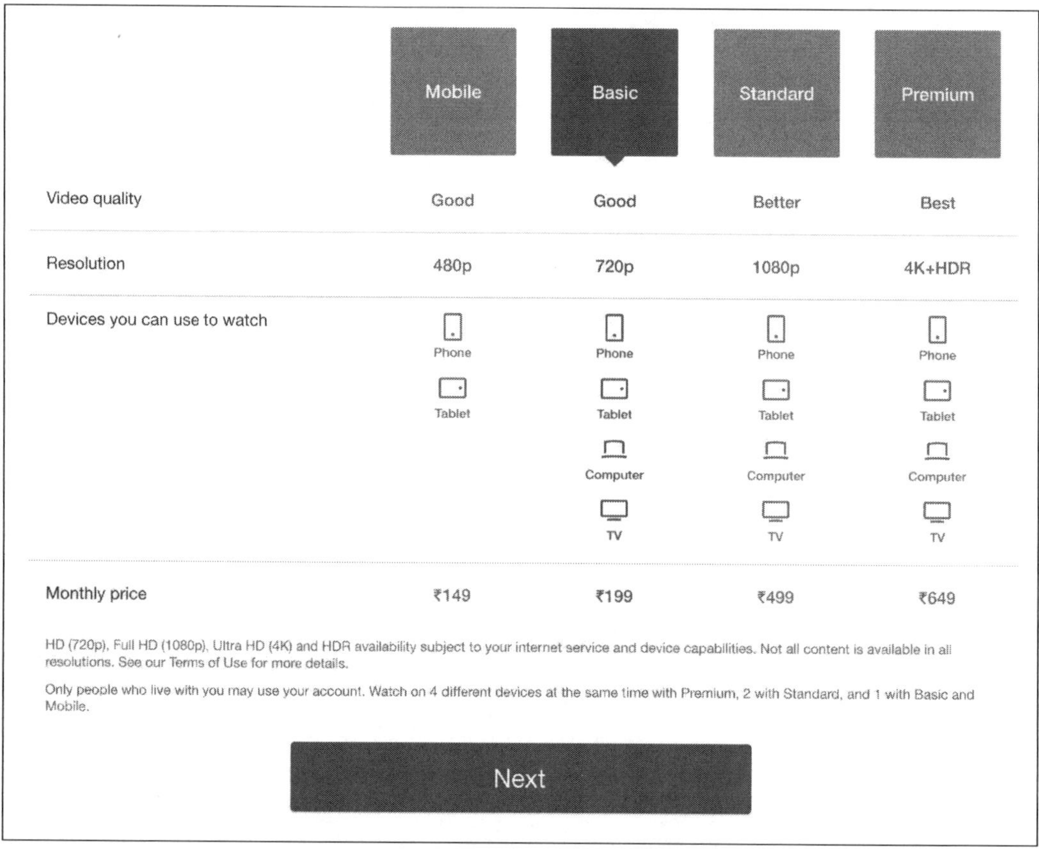

	Mobile	Basic	Standard	Premium
Video quality	Good	Good	Better	Best
Resolution	480p	720p	1080p	4K+HDR
Devices you can use to watch	Phone	Phone Tablet Computer TV	Phone Tablet Computer TV	Phone Tablet Computer TV
Monthly price	₹149	₹199	₹499	₹649

Figure 2.12: Netflix plans on subscribe page

Conclusion

We should hold the view that achieving a better user experience does not solely rely on offering fewer choices but rather on strategically placing and timing these choices. It is imperative to understand how choices and their associated response times fit into the context of your service or product to foster a meaningful connection and engagement with your users.

While there are numerous web design guidelines and best practices to adhere to, they often converge on a central principle. Avoid adding unnecessary complexity to the already intricate lives of your users.

In the next chapter, we will discuss about the Miller's law. It is a law of memory of magical number 7, It conveys that a human can remember only 7 +- numbers max without practice. We will discuss Miller's law as well as the things we use and experience in daily life. We will also explore how it impacts the decisions we take while developing a design or layout for the users.

Join our book's Discord space

Join the book's Discord Workspace for Latest updates, Offers, Tech happenings around the world, New Release and Sessions with the Authors:

https://discord.bpbonline.com

CHAPTER 3
Miller's Law

"The average person can only keep 7 (plus or minus 2) items in their working memory."

Introduction

An average human can hold approximately seven (plus or minus two) items in their working memory. In other words, people can effectively process and remember around 5 to 9 pieces of information at a time.

This concept is often referred to as *Miller's 7± 2* and has significant implications in various fields, including psychology, cognitive science, and **user experience (UX)** design. Understanding this limitation of working memory capacity is crucial for designing interfaces and communication materials that are user-friendly and do not overwhelm individuals with too much information at once.

In UX design, for example, adhering to Miller's Law means that designers should consider the limited capacity of users' working memory when presenting information. To enhance user comprehension and retention, designers often aim to simplify content, break it into smaller, digestible chunks, and use clear and concise language. By doing so, they can make it easier for users to process and remember the information presented, ultimately improving the overall user experience. In this chapter, you will be introduced to Miller's law in such a manner that you will be able to observe the usage of Miller's law in your day to day life. You will also understand how Miller's law impacts the design decision taken by you and how to make the user's life easier by applying Miller's law and reducing cognitive load.

Structure

In this chapter, we will cover the following topics:

- History
- Understanding Miller's law with examples
- How does Miller's law impact the design?

Objectives

In this chapter, you will understand the limitations of human memory and the value of magic number 7. You will also understand how Miller's Magic Number 7 rule is applied in real-world examples. This will help you observe the things around you to relate to this psychological law of Magic Number 7. Miller's Magic Number 7 psychological law is going to help you understand the limits of human memory and how to use this information in your real life and live projects. By the end of this chapter, you will learn how to make it easier for the users to memorize more than 7 numbers. We have also included some live examples which you might not have noticed earlier but follows Miller's rule.

History

In 1956, the psychologist and researcher *George A. Miller* conducted a study, aiming to identify what he believed to be the boundary of human information processing capacity. As a notable finding, he observed that most individuals could effectively retain approximately 7 items, give, or take 2, in their short-term memory.

Surpassing this threshold posed significant challenges for individuals trying to commit information to memory. This phenomenon was particularly critical for those encountering the information for the first time, as they had not yet had the opportunity to encode it into their long-term memory.

Given the limitations of human short-term memory, it is advisable for web designers to tailor the volume of information presented to website visitors accordingly. Adhering to Miller's Law holds particular significance for contemporary UX designers, as web users tend to be averse to information overload.

Understanding Miller's law with examples

Let us begin this section by playing a game.

Read the given words, carefully in one go with the aim of retaining as many of them as you can in your memory:

- Dog
- Diary
- Table
- Mango
- Cycle
- Plants
- Banana
- Onion
- Chair
- Bottle
- Pen
- Water

Try to recall as many items from the list as you can without referring to them. How many could you recall? Try a similar exercise with a few more people around you. You will be surprised to see the result. It is worth noting that most individuals can typically remember 5 to 9 items.

John Miller's psychological law, also known as the *Magic Number Seven rule,* suggests that humans can hold approximately 7 ± 2 of information in their short-term memory.

Now, let us try another exercise.

All you need to do is read this given number twice. Cover the number with your hand, and try and repeat it.

The number is 8810987563.

Did you try remembering? Did you do it in one go?

Now let us try the same exercise again:

8810 - 9875 – 63

Read twice, cover the number with your hand, and try to repeat it with your memory.

Was it not easier this time? Did you notice the difference?

This is the same number but broken into three chunks. This is exactly what John Miller's Law tries to convey

A human mind has a limitation for memorizing the stuff they see in their memory, and that limit is 7 ± 2. This is the magic number 7 rule. To make it simpler, we may say a human mind can memorize 5 to 9 pieces of information easily. More than that can be done through practice or by breaking them into chunks.

Overview of a chunk

Chunk is exactly what you did in the above exercise to memorize the number 3810987563 as 3810 - 9875 - 63. You could memorize this 10-digit number because it was broken into three chunks. So, for you, it was three chunks to remember. Chunks are broken pieces that let your working memory memorize things naturally.

Remember how you memorize a mobile number? In India, a mobile number is 10 digits, and you never memorize those 10 digits separately. With your unconscious mind, you break those into 3 or 4 chunks to memorize. Observe a few people telling their own mobile number, and you will realize how they chunked their own mobile number so that it is a part of their working memory.

Now, I am sure you will observe people saying a bigger number, like their mobile number, PAN number (in India, as shown in *Figure 3.1*), Social Security number (used in the USA, as shown in *Figure 3.2*), or any other bigger digit number.

Let us observe a live example of this. Notice the social security number and credit card (refer to *Figure 3.1* and *Figure 3.2*) numbers in the above screens; these are 8 and 16-digit numbers respectively, that look like they exceed the limit of human memory. That is why these are intentionally placed in 3-4-3-4 chunks with 2-4 digits in each chunk to make it easier to read and memorize. This is a normal practice being used in many countries. Make sure you do the same when writing a number on your UI screen or web page.

Figure 3.1: Social Security Number

Figure 3.2: Credit card

These are the live examples that you can observe around you in the objects you have been using. Now let us look at a few examples in the digital world that use Miller's law.

Refer to *Figure 3.3*, which is from one of the biggest streaming platforms, Netflix:

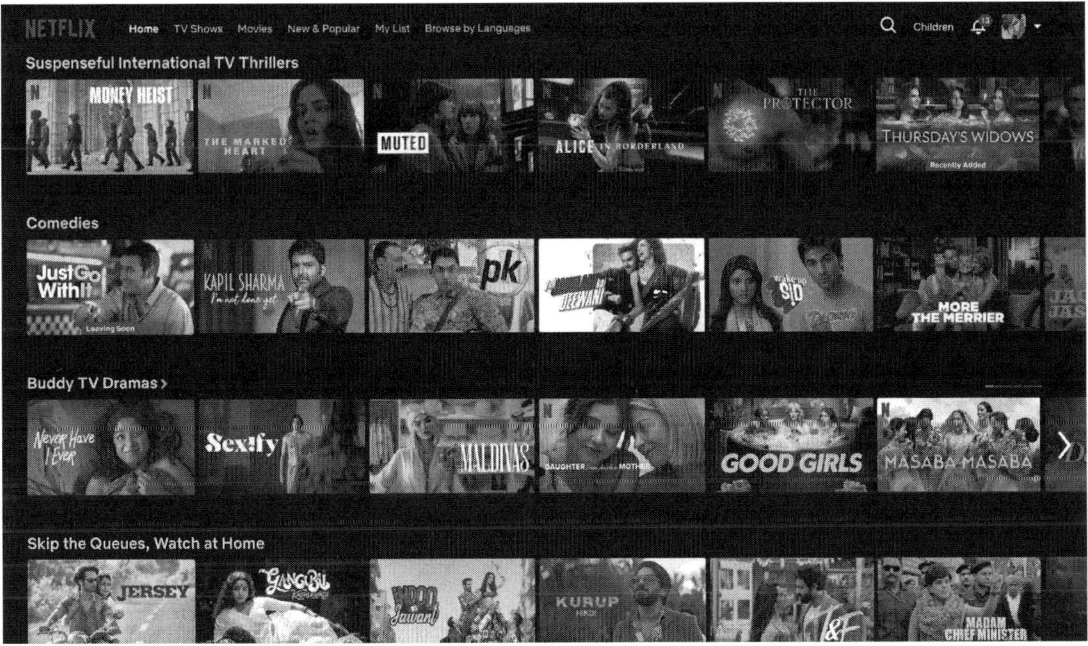

Figure 3.3: Netflix: Post-login homepage

In today's world, people spend a lot of time on online movies/shows streaming platforms to look for the movies of their choice. It has been observed that people spend a lot of time browsing through the options and take a lot of time deciding what to watch today. Here, Netflix does an amazing job of reducing the cognitive load and arranging the options in such a manner that it helps the users narrow down their search and conclude with one option to watch on a particular day.

The first thing you will see is that Netflix has a maximum of six movies or show options visible to you on one single screen. You can scroll through and see more if you wish to, but it is easier to notice when these options are a maximum of 7±2, They have tried implementing Miller's law very beautifully to help the users memorize the options given on their Web / TV screen.

Another observation is that they have chunks of different kinds of movies separated into different categories. It is possible for a few shows to be available in two categories as well. They kept category names like suspenseful international TV thrillers, comedies, and so on. in such a manner that it will match user's choice even if it is repeated. This helps the users find their desired movies easily. It is also easier to recall which movie they have seen in which row/section.

Walmart is known for selling anything and everything you can imagine, and that is why their website's information architecture has become very challenging.

Refer to *Figure 3.4*, This is a great example of handling a complex information architecture with the help of Miller's law. Walmart has strategically introduced a few chunks to differentiate their categories. Left part of the column shows the main categories, and when you hover on any of those categories, you will see another subcategory of the selected category. This adds another layer of visual imagery.

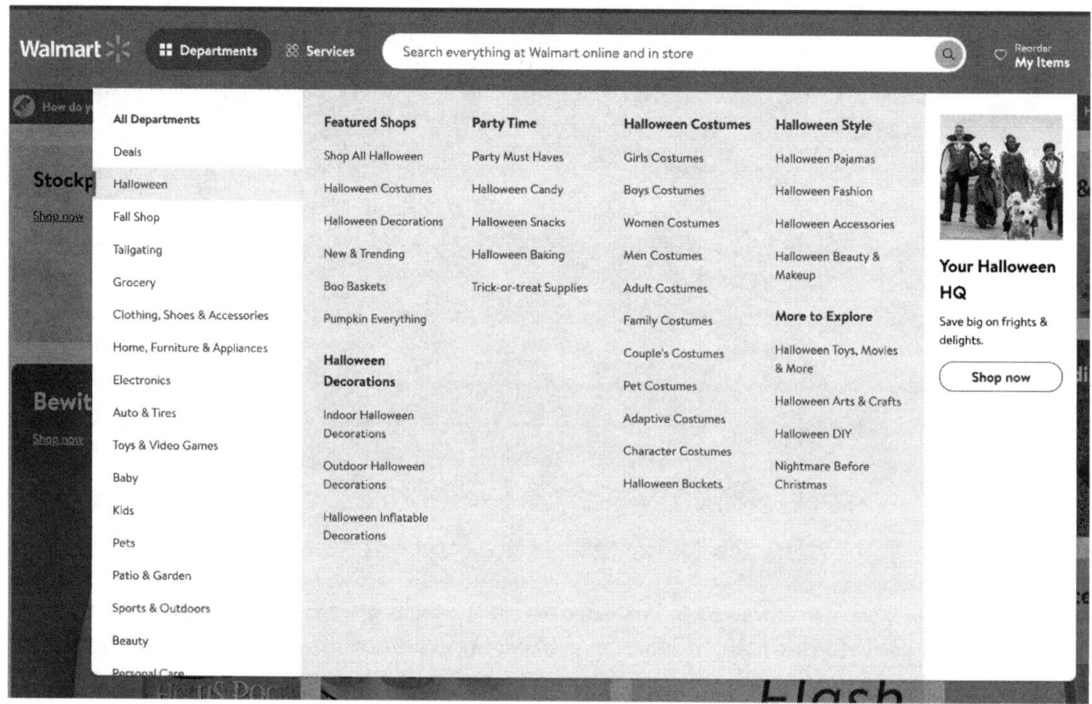

Figure 3.4: Walmart Website Navigation: Mega menu

Here the chunks are also differentiated with the help of background color and highlighting the category and sub-category name by making it bold. As well as the image shown at the top right (refer to *Figure 3.4*, Walmart mega menu), this is another easy way to showcase one of the chunks.

Usually, the information on such websites is very dense, but with the help of Miller's theory, it has been easier to scan and read.

Now, let us look at a website that people visit when they are in need of inspiration, Pinterest. Refer to *Figure 3.5* to check the explore section of the Pinterest website:

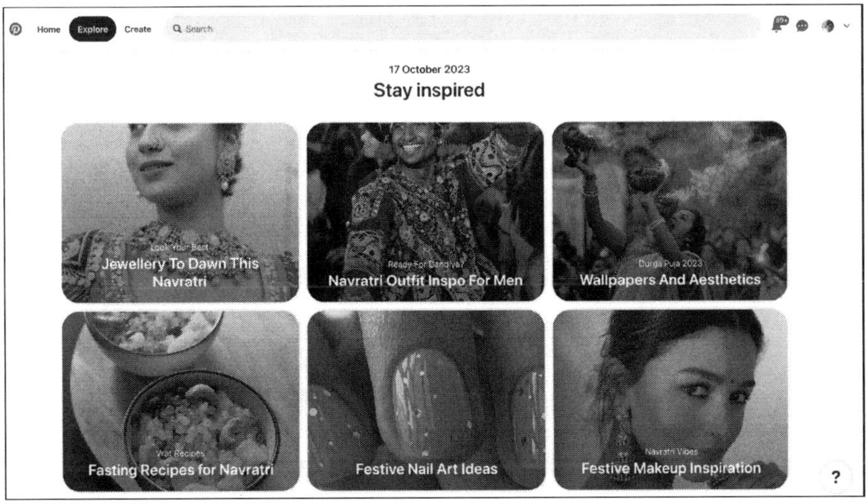

Figure 3.5: Pinterest Website: Explore section

People visit Pinterest when they seek inspiration in any field; that means it is a bank of information/picture of most possible topics. Now that there is such a huge amount of information, the challenge is how to show it to the users, and make it easy to scan, search, and reach the desired content as soon as possible.

The Explore page of Pinterest has the data arranged in multiple chunks. In fact, they made some sub-categories or, as you may call them, chunks within the chunks, to make it easier to browse.

Their first chunk is date. They are conveying the recency of the information, which means the information is being presented in the sequence of being added today vs. yesterday or any other date. And within a date, they have Chunks as categories, which is like, jewelry to draw in Navaratri, festive makeup inspiration, and so on.

As a user, now it is easier to find information since it will stay in our memory with an extra layer of information which is date. Date will always help me recall this information / Pinterest board. Because the date is helping you arrange the information in multiple number of groups / chunks. With the help of arranging the information in chunks, it will help a reader or content consumer consume the information without much cognitive load.

By now, you must have understood the value of Miller's law in your design and how it helps the users escape this cognitive pressure and focus on things easily. Let us shift our focus towards day-to-day activities and the stuff that you use very often.

There are a few examples that you should observe and use in your real life to make sure you do not struggle to remember the presented options or steps.

- **Phone contact list**: Imagine a mobile phone contact list. Instead of displaying an endless list of contacts, a well-designed interface will typically show around 5 to 9 contacts per screen. This allows users to easily scan and remember the names and details of the people they are looking for, in line with Miller's law.

- **Navigation menus**: Website or app navigation menus often follow Miller's law by limiting the number of top-level menu items to around 5 to 7. This makes it easier for users to find their way around and remember the available options.

- **Supermarket shelves**: In a supermarket, products are organized into categories, and each category may contain around 5 to 9 different brands or variations of a product. This organization aligns with Miller's Law, making it easier for shoppers to make choices.

- **Musical chords**: Musicians often work with chord progressions that consist of around 7 notes or chords. This number aligns with Miller's law and helps musicians remember and work with musical sequences.

- **TV remote control**: The buttons on a TV remote control are typically limited to a small number of essential functions, such as volume, channel, power, and maybe a few others. This limitation adheres to Miller's Law, allowing users to operate their devices without feeling overwhelmed by options.

- **Presentation slides**: When creating presentation slides, it is recommended to keep the number of bullet points or key messages on a single slide to 5-7 points. This ensures that the audience can absorb and remember the information more effectively.

Conclusion

Clearly, there are many similarities between psychology and UX, and Miller's law serves as a great illustration of this connection. Violating this principle leads to a subpar experience for online audiences, emphasizing the importance of implementing chunking (The process of dividing the content in multiple chunks/groups) to facilitate effortless content scanning and retention. Keep in mind that presenting seven products per page or dividing content into seven menu sections is not obligatory, as the main goal is to ensure that users can easily view products/items without burdening them with the need to memorize information.

I hold the view that achieving a better user experience does not solely rely on offering fewer choices but rather on strategically placing and timing these choices. It is imperative to understand how choices and their associated response times fit into the context of your service or product to foster a meaningful connection and engagement with your users.

While there are numerous web design guidelines and best practices to adhere to, they often converge on a central principle such as avoid adding unnecessary complexity to the already intricate lives of your users.

In the next chapter, we are going to discuss about Jakob's law, which helps us consider the conventional methods. It refers to the fact that it is better to choose a familiar way of design because people relate more with familiarity. This will be discussed in detail in the next chapter.

CHAPTER 4
Jakob's Law

*"Law of familiarity - It's always better to choose
usual design solutions that are familiar to users."*

Introduction

Jakob's Law, derived from natural principles, revolves around embracing a language that
adheres to familiar web patterns and conventions. This principle was introduced by Jakob
Nielsen, a prominent figure in human-computer interaction research, often referred to as
the **king of usability**. Nielsen's work garnered significant media attention, leading him
to co-establish the renowned usability consulting firm, Nielsen Norman Group, alongside
fellow usability expert *Donald Norman*.

According to Jakob's law of the internet user experience, users typically allocate most of
their online time to other websites rather than yours. Consequently, users prefer when your
website functions similarly to the other familiar sites they frequent. Therefore, designing
in accordance with established patterns that users are already accustomed to, is crucial.

Drawing from prior experiences, users tend to carry their expectations from one familiar
context to another. Introducing new and unconventional elements on your website can
potentially bewilder and disorient your customers. By leveraging existing mental models,
we can craft user experiences that enable them to concentrate on their objectives, rather
than grappling with unfamiliar concepts. Mitigate discrepancies by employing a shared
design language that users readily recognize.

Structure

This chapter is going to focus on how familiarity helps the users act fast and complete the desired task with zero or very small learning curve. How it makes the users more comfortable with your design / website / app. Since the wheel is a proven instrument in transportation, this chapter will discuss why we would need to reinvent the wheel. We will also discuss when to reinvent and how to make your design different from the conventions already in the market.

This chapter, moreover, covers the following topics:

- History of Jakob's law
- Usage of Jakob's law and its usage
- Tips and strategies to use Jakob's law

Objectives

Jakob's rule of familiarity is going to help you plan your design in terms of making it similar to the apps / websites your users use or plan a different design where there is a real need for it. After this chapter, you will be able to decide how much inspiration is good to follow and when to make a drastic change.

History

Jakob's law was recommended by *Jakob Nielsen*. He has a doctorate in usability pioneer. He pioneered usability practices, commencing his work in 1983. He currently serves as the principal at Nielsen Norman Group, a firm he co-founded alongside *Dr. Donald A. Norman*, former Vice President of Research at Apple Inc. *Dr. Nielsen* was instrumental in promoting the **discount usability engineering** approach for swift and cost-effective enhancements of user interfaces. He is credited with inventing various usability techniques, notably heuristic evaluation. His contributions extend to holding 79 United States patents, primarily focused on simplifying internet usage.

Jakob Nielsen has been lauded as:

- *"…the king of usability* (Internet Magazine)
- *"…the guru of web page usability* (The New York Times)
- *"…the next best thing to a true time machine* (USA Today)
- *"…the smartest person on the web* (ZDNet AnchorDesk)
- *"…the world's leading expert on web usability* (U.S. News & World Report)
- *"…one of the top 10 minds in small business* (FORTUNE Small Business)
- *"…the world's leading expert on user-friendly design* (Stuttgarter Zeitung, Germany)

- *"…knows more about what makes Web sites work than anyone else on the planet* (Chicago Tribune)

(Source: **Nielsen Norman Group** website: **https://www.nngroup.com/**)

In a nutshell, this rule says:

Human beings are complex creatures. We have a natural tendency to be curious and explorative, yet we also find considerable solace in familiar experiences.

There are some important aspects to keep in mind:

Being a designer, you must be doing a lot of competitive analysis for the product you are going to build or the product problem you are going to solve. It is the general consensus and part of the UX and design process that we must do competitive analysis to know more about the competitors, define the benchmark, and get some inspiration from the competition if needed.

But the question is, does this process always help you to set the benchmark? Is this the bare minimum level of solution that you need to figure out? Or do you end up getting inspired by your competition's solutions or visual design language? The answer is yes. I have seen designers get inspired by a few solutions, visual language and end up copying a few of the stuff. But is that a problem?

As a UX designer myself, meeting with small business founders and their designers is very frequent. The designers in those organizations always complain that we do not get enough time to research and do the complete UX process and end up copying the industry leaders or mixing and matching with a few industry leading apps / websites and building something like those. They even get inspired by the color theme and visual style sometimes.

But the question is, why do your business stakeholders or founders ask you to copy so. Try to understand the reason behind this. Empathy is not for just the users, you should also try to empathize with your stakeholders, business folks, PMs, and Dev to understand their challenges. Then you will be able to give them a confident solution.

The following could be the possible reasons why they ask you to follow the existing trends and design similar to existing products:

- Being industry leaders, they have done deeper research with the resources they have, and a small business might not have that much time and resources to put on a similar problem statement.

- A small business founder believes in the solution a bigger organization or competition has taken.

- Or since the users are using the competition's app or website and they are already familiar with those digital solutions, it seems like a clever idea to use a similar solution and offer it to the same users because you are going to try to acquire those users to your platform, but you will try to have just some differentiating factors so that users have a reason to switch to your app or website.

Reason number three is Jakob's law of familiarity. Since the users are already familiar with some website or app, they will easily become familiar with your app or website and will complete certain tasks in a quicker manner because they have a very limited learning curve.

Now going back to the question posed before, does competition analysis make sense, and when do we need to do competitive analysis exactly? If we do competitive analysis as the very first process, the designer might get biased and end up copying the already better solutions and visual ideas. In case, we plan to check the competition after having thought of solution, there is a big risk that the competition might have solved the problem in a better manner, or their visual and UX solutions are way better than the solution I have thought of.

Here is my take on this; in my eyes, as experienced designers, it is our duty to check the competition before we start thinking of the solution so that we can set a solution benchmark in our minds, while also not letting ourselves be biased towards the solution they have offered. Then it is time to figure out the use cases that are not covered in the competition's solutions and simultaneously improve that as well. Now keeping this in mind while exploring solutions.

How is your solution better than others. You may test if with some user research as well as with quick *click test* or *AB testing* with your real users and then go live confidently.

Jakob's law and its usage

Let us look at the top navigation panels of few of the world's most well-known e-commerce websites:

Refer to *Figure 4.1*, for the top navigation panel of Walmart's website:

Figure 4.1: Walmart website's top navigation

Refer to *Figure 4.2* for the navigation panel of Alibaba's website:

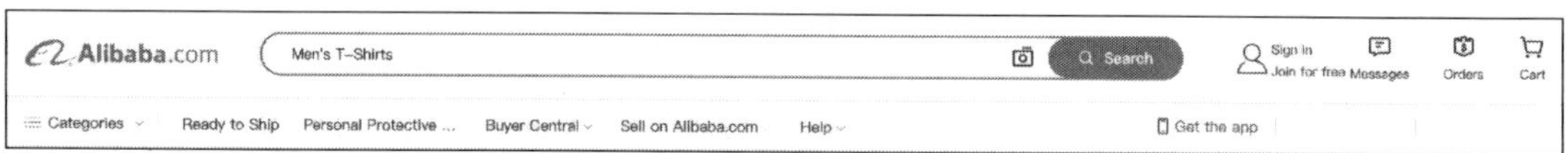

Figure 4.2: Alibaba website's top navigation

Refer to *Figure 4.3* for the top navigation panel of Amazon's website:

Figure 4.3: *Amazon website's top navigation*

Refer to *Figure 4.4* for the top navigation panel of Asos's website:

Figure 4.4: *Asos website's top navigation*

Refer to *Figure 4.5*, for the top navigation panel of Flipkart's website:

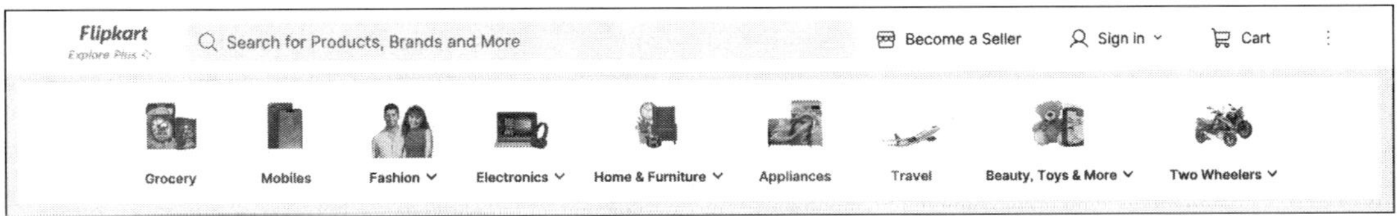

Figure 4.5: *Flipkart website's top navigation*

Refer to *Figure 4.6*, for the top navigation panel of Myntra's website:

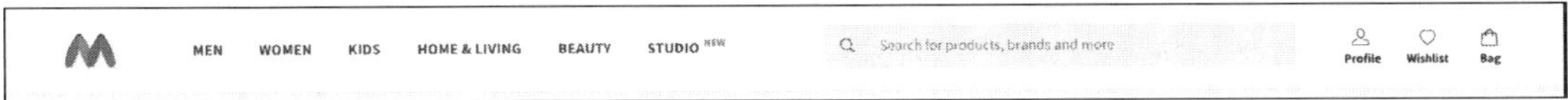

Figure 4.6: *Myntra website top navigation*

Did you observe some similarities in very different e-commerce websites that are meant for different countries but have the same purpose of buying stuff online.

Now observe the common items in all the above top navigation you will notice. During online shopping, users anticipate the following:

- The logo positioned on the left (it assures that they are at the correct store),
- The search bar centered while being the most prominent element (it facilitates finding what the user needs quickly),
- List of the categories to explore in case the user does not want to Start with a Search Bar,
- Account login located on the right (this speeds up the checkout process),
- Shopping cart situated to the right (it enables a swift checkout)

In a few online shopping (e-commerce) website or apps you may find a symbol of a bag instead of a cart icon, but the overall experience and expectation remain the same.

This is the benefit of following Jakob's law of familiarity, that users find all e-shopping websites familiar, and they do not struggle to find what they are looking for even if they switch stores. There is a level of consistently among all websites.

The law does not mandate complete uniformity across all websites and experiences. Rather, it emphasizes the necessity of certain similarities. For instance, the placement of the search button/option on a webpage follows a general pattern. Typically, this feature is situated in the top-right corner or centered at the top. Deviating from this norm by relocating it to the left corner or elsewhere on the site can perplex users accustomed to the standard placement. Therefore, it is vital to remember this principle during project development.

A shared design language implies creating designs based on the established patterns and norms with which users are already familiar. Discover how we integrate these standard languages into adaptable design systems with our comprehensive guide on developing design systems.

These established patterns and norms extend beyond the realm of online platforms; they permeate various aspects of our physical environment. To illustrate this point, consider a real-life instance of Jakob's law:

- Consider the universally recognized traffic light system. We all understand that a red light signifies **stop**, while a green light means **go**. But imagine if a city were to reverse this arrangement, making red mean **go** and green signify **stop**. Such a deviation would undoubtedly cause confusion and frustration and, in this scenario, pose a significant danger.

- Another case in point, is when in 2016, over a million Jeep, Dodge, and Chrysler vehicles were recalled due to a departure from a common design language. General motors faced substantial issues when it altered the functioning of the shifting mechanism in certain vehicles, resulting in an **unintuitive** design that provided inadequate tactile and visual feedback, leading to numerous accidents.

A point to remember is:

Convention is the best friend of UX designers.

When you cannot figure out a better solution, it is always advisable to go with the convention, and that is the safer option than having a suboptimal solution unless you have the time and resources to try out your with a few users, run an experiment (AB test/ click test, etc.), or you are planning to have an exceptionally different solution and test it out to stand out of the crowd.

Now let us observe an example from the non-online world. Have you observed the gear box of the manual cars and noticed the placement of all the gears, including the reverse gear (refer to *Figures 4.7* and *4.8*):

Figure 4.7: *Manual car gear box*

Figure 4.8: *Manual car gear box*

If you pick any manual car of any brand, you will not see the change in the placement of the gear, wiper, or indicator light switch. These are shared knowledge or shared designs that everyone is trained with. The moment you try to change this convention, it will cause a lot of accidents because there will be a learning curve for every car model or car brand. So, now, if you ignore Jakob's law of familiarity, it may cause a big loss and a lot of confusion within the car for the driver, and consequentially lead to multiple accidents.

However, there are a few scenarios where brands want to introduce a new look or revamp the style of their own old product, and for this, they need to change a few conventions. Now the question is, *should we do that or not. Let users change their behavior and adapt to new things, or let users decide when they want to move to a new design?*

A classic example of a similar use case is the **Gmail** design revamp (refer to *Figure 4.9*). A few years ago, Google planned to change GMail's complete look and feel of the inbox and introduce a few new features like social and promotional tabs to help users filter their important e-mails:

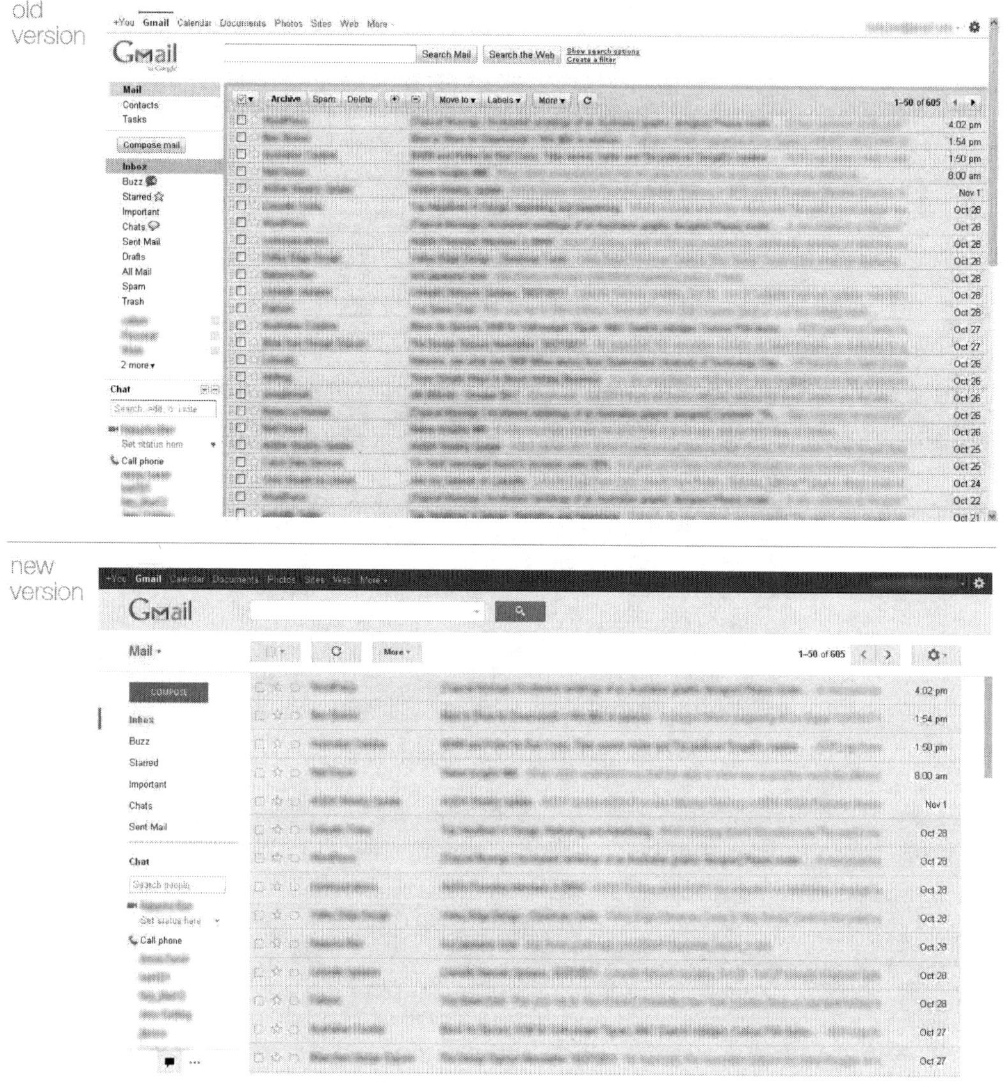

Figure 4.9: *Gmail's old vs. new version*

Google took this strong decision to change the complete look with a few enhanced features but did not implement it for everyone overnight. Initially, they launched this new look and sent a notification to everyone to switch to the newer look by highlighting the benefits of the newer layout. Later, they released the new look for a few and asked them to switch back to the older version if they were not comfortable.

With this attempt, users did not panic to see this new change because they had the option to switch to an older version when they wanted. Users got enough time to get comfortable with the new look, and Google handled it very well by guiding their users to adopt the change according to their comfort.

Tips and strategies to use Jakob's Law

- **Following are some tips to use Jakob's Law:** Encourage users to concentrate on products, services, offers, and other content, rather than intricate and imaginative UX innovations.

- **Terminology and labeling**: Employ language and terms that resonate with your audience, even if they differ from your own preferences.

- **Information organization and navigation**: Construct a content framework that can be swiftly comprehended and effortlessly traversed by your intended audience.

- **Maintain equilibrium**: Websites overloaded with creativity and non-standard elements can bewilder users. Strive to limit the presence of unfamiliar elements.

- **Assist users**: Offer them guidance for navigating non-obvious patterns.

- **Exceed expectations**: Empower users to have full control over your website. Let their expectations be met, fostering trust and the likelihood of return visits.

- **Respect users' experiences**: Consider prior user experiences, giving them prominence, and utilizing them. This approach is often superior to creating something entirely new merely for the sake of differentiation.

Conclusion

It is always better to choose usual design solutions that are familiar to users, because users feel familiar and comfortable interacting with such designs. Do not try to reinvent the wheel.

For example, apart from providing entertaining content, YouTube demonstrated astuteness by allowing users to choose whether to adopt or decline new designs without implementing substantial alterations. Similarly, Gmail also waited for the users to adapt to a new design language or switch back to an older design when they revamped the complete website. Furthermore, they consistently request user feedback to enhance the quality of new designs.

So, by adhering to Jakob's law in the process of designing your website or app does not imply that every website and app should start looking similar to each other, but try not to change the conventional methods, shared knowledge and design, and the habits of your users. These kinds of changes bring a lot of discomfort to users' mental model, and you will experience a lot of drop-offs in your user journey.

In this chapter, we focused on making things easier for the user by using conventional methods and familiar design, and in the next chapter, we are going to discuss why you should not make your designs very easy because it involves confusion for the users.

Let us go to the next chapter, where you will understand that if you simplify too much, that will also cause a problem for the users.

Join our book's Discord space

Join the book's Discord Workspace for Latest updates, Offers, Tech happenings around the world, New Release and Sessions with the Authors:

https://discord.bpbonline.com

CHAPTER 5
Tesler's Law

*"**Law of conservation of complexity:***
If you simplify too much, you will transfer some complexity to the users."

Introduction

Tesler, known for his contributions to computer science, highlighted that each application possesses a fundamental level of complexity that cannot be eliminated entirely. Rather, the question remains: who will shoulder this complexity, the user, application developer, or platform developer?

Simplifying things is not a simple task. Often, the most user-friendly products are the result of extensive labor and meticulous fine-tuning. Crafting a *simple* product demands substantial effort. As we reduce complexity for users, we are essentially transferring the weight onto designers, developers, and other involved parties.

Tesler's law serves as a guide for making informed design decisions that strike a balance between the inherent complexity of software systems and the need to prioritize individual requirements and usability. By adopting this approach, designers can enhance the overall quality of user experiences.

And, as designers, developers, or product managers, it is our duty to bear this responsibility, ensuring that our users encounter the best possible experience.

Tesler's law helps in the following manners while designing:

- Prioritize user needs

- Maintain balance between simplicity and functionality

- Establish reasonable expectations

- Prioritize effective task completion

Complexity behaves akin to energy—it cannot be generated or eliminated, merely shifted elsewhere. Every product comes with an inherent amount of irreducible complexity; the only question to be answered is, who is going to deal with it, the designer, the developer, or the user?

Structure

In this chapter, we are going to discuss the irreducible complexity that every product has and whether the complexity should be reduced, removed, or transferred. The chapter will discuss the following topics:

- History

- Real-life examples of Tesler's law

- Tips to use Tesler's law

Objectives

Tesler's law of conservation of complexity is the perfect law for you to practice and deal with. A designer has to build a lot of products from scratch, which could be a complex user story to be solved or an existing complex product that needs to be simplified. It is important to know how much complexity should be handled by designers and how much a user should be handling.

History

Larry Tesler, a computer scientist with a focus on human-computer interaction, boasts a career spanning *Xerox PARC, Apple, Amazon,* and *Yahoo.* In the mid-1980s, *Tesler* outlined a principle, contending that *complexity does not vanish but instead migrates from one domain to another.* When streamlining the system for users, the intricacy inherently shifts to the developers and designers. *Tesler* is the personality who conceived of the idea of copying and pasting. He only came up with this law of complexity in the mid-1980s.

As per *Dan Saffer's* interview with *Larry Tesler* in *Designing for Interaction; In the early stages of their (Dan Saffer & Larry Tesler) field, during Tesler's tenure at Xerox PARC,* the concept of user interface consistency was both groundbreaking and contentious. Many of the folks recognized that fostering consistency could yield advantages not only for users but also for developers, as standards could be encapsulated in shared software libraries. They presented an economic rationale: by establishing standards and promoting consistency, they presented that they could decrease time to market and code size.

It has been hypothesized that every application inherently carries a certain level of irreducible complexity, with the key question being who would bear the responsibility of managing it.

Given that computers in that era were small, slow, and expensive, programs were designed to be compact rather than user-friendly. Users had to contend with complexity because the programmer could not. However, commercial software is crafted once and employed millions of times. If a million users each spend a minute daily grappling with complexity that an engineer could have eradicated in a week by adding a bit more complexity to the software, it amounts to penalizing the user for the sake of making the engineer's job more convenient.

Real-life examples of Tesler's law

Tesler's law is applied to the products we use in our day-to-day life. Let us understand how this actually works on any of the products complexity in terms of transferring the complexity to the user vs. the product makers.

If you notice the following *Figure 5.1*, it conveys that the complexity of the product can be transferred from user to designer to make The user feel a bit easier to use. It is the responsibility of the designer to transfer less of the complexity to the user and keep most of that for themselves.

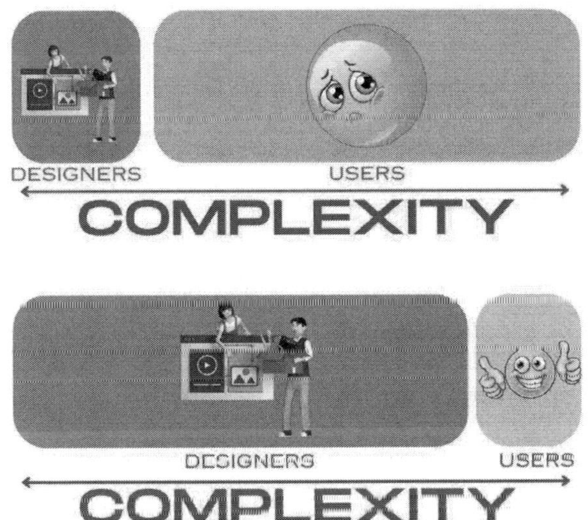

Figure 5.1: Transferring the complexity from users to designers

There are a few real-life examples from which we may observe how complexity is being transferred.

Imagine a road that is full of traffic. We see most of the bigger cities in the world struggling with the complexity of handling dense populations and, hence, traffic on the road.

In the next section, we will discuss a few solutions to this complexity that we may observe around us.

Traffic lights

Traffic is being handled by introducing some rules around red, green, and orange lights to help users be disciplined. This rule of traffic being handled by respective lights makes the process a bit easier. Refer to *Figure 5.2*, which depicts traffic signal lights.

If you notice here, the complexity of handling traffic is something that the average user (driver) has to do, but some of that complexity has been transferred to the system via automating the lighting system to organize and divide the traffic within a limited interval of time. Since the complexity cannot be completely removed from the users, it is diverted to the system so that users will face less complexity.

Figure 5.2: Traffic lights and traffic

Flyovers and Bridge

Another example of handling traffic is the construction of flyovers and bridges so that traffic is diverted, and the movement of the vehicle gets smoother. With the help of the system, more of the real estate has been used, and height has increased since there's limited available space on the ground at a particular place or junction. With the help of flyovers, a few of the vehicles are able to move without interfering with each other or blocking each other's way. Refer to *Figure 5.3* with a set of flyovers to handle the traffic.

If you look at this flyover example (as shown in the following figure) through the lens of Tesler's law, you will notice that there are a lot of complexities to handling the traffic that was being handled by the users / drivers of the vehicles. With the help of flyovers, designers and engineers diverted that complexity to the system and constructed the flyover so that the users had less complexity to deal with. It will not remove complete traffic definitely, but it will reduce the users' complexity and make their driving experience smoother for them.

Figure 5.3: Flyovers to deal with heavy traffic

DSLR cameras

Have you noticed the DSLR camera that is used to click exceptional photos and shoot videos? It has many options to enhance the picture quality and controls to change as per the background and lighting you have to shoot in. If you understand all those technical jargons and you have the fundamental knowledge of lights, aperture, angles, etc., it is a great asset for you to deal with and click the exceptional picture of your choice. Refer to *Figure 5.4* (DSLR camera).

Figure 5.4: DSLR photo / video camera with lots of functions

On the other hand, if you do not understand the technicalities, these functions might be a slightly complex for you. To deal with the technicalities, DSLR cameras have given you the option of auto mode. The camera adjusts all the technical functionality as per the lighting, color, aperture, etc. and tries to give you the best possible result with the auto mode pictures.

Here are two points to bring to your attention:

- With the help of Auto Mode, a lot of the complexity has been transferred to the system, leaving very little for the users to deal with if you are an immature photographer.

- However, if you are an expert and professional photographer, you will never go with the auto mode and will adjust all the features as per your understanding because a professional photographer understands very well how to deal with functionalities to get the best out of them.

In short, complexities could be a time taking issue that the users would need to deal with. If users do love and use that particular product and they love the complexity, they know well how to deal with this complexity because they are the subject matter experts. So, if you remove all the functionalities and have only auto mode in your DSLR camera, I am sure it is not going to be the favorite option for all professional photographers.

Deal with the complexities very subjectively and after understanding the joy of your users.

Adobe Photoshop

One of the most popular tools for photo editing and designing is Adobe Photoshop. Similar to DSLR cameras, Photoshop (photo editing software) has a lot of features that enable designers to enhance the quality of a picture or change a few properties of the picture and achieve the expected outcome. Because of its vast level of photo editing options, photographers can change the complete look and feel of their photograph, edit something that is not clicked at all, or merge multiple photographs to make a single one. Similarly, editing is possible with the help of Adobe Photoshop. This software is also used to design the layouts of any product, and different kinds of designers use it for different purposes.

Now, if you look at Photoshop as software, it seems a bit complex, having so many layers, tools, functions, etc., and one needs good training to achieve a great outcome with this software. Refer to *Figure 5.5* below, which shows a lot of functionalities for editing the pictures.

There are a few functionalities that auto correct the colors and contrast in your photograph that are for new users However, those are few because Photoshop was developed keeping in mind enthusiastic photo editors, and they need a lot of freedom to change the current photograph. With the help of extraordinary features, it is possible for them to generate a completely different outcome compared to what the original picture is.

Figure 5.5: Adobe Photoshop software with a lot of image and color change options

So, in this example of Photoshop, you will realize that most of the complexity is not transferred to the system, and it is not made to be easy with just a few selective options. Here, the use case is different. Here, Tesler's law is being used in a limited quantity and is very precarious because if the options to play with the images are not there, none of the photographers, editors, and designers are going to love this software.

Another example we may think of is games (mobile games, PC games, or console games). Gamers love the games because they are pushing their boundaries to win. It is challenging and complex sometimes and has a lot of other angles of gamification, but fundamentally, if Tesler's law were applied in games and the games were made simple, most of the complexity would have been transferred to the system, and gamers (refer to *Figure 5.6*) will not be enjoying their game and challenging themselves.

Figure 5.6: A gamer is playing a game with multiple platforms

Just imagine if the games were simple; the gamers would lose interest very quickly because there is no sense of achievement after achieving a particular goal or completing a particular level. Gamers do enjoy the game because they gamers feel very high level of motivation when they fail multiple times, try hard, figure out some way to win and then apply some strategic planning to win a battle. This is the sense of achievement, and it calls for a celebration.

So, be careful when you want to apply Tesler's law and how much complexity should be removed. You are not supposed to remove all the complexity from the user and pass it all to the system. That may also fail in a lot of cases. You should empathize with your users very deeply and understand their motivation before you work on the user journey. Few users love the complexity, but a few are in need of a simple flow and journey. At the same time, a few products are very complex in nature, and you cannot remove the complexity completely. So, you may target transferring most of the complexity to the system and as little as possible to the users so that they will love to use your app.

Tips to use Tesler's law

The following are the tips to use Tesler's law:

- Shift the primary responsibility away from users during the system's development and design phases.

- Avoid excessive simplification. Completely eliminating complexity from a product is unattainable. However, by streamlining the system, you inadvertently heighten the challenges involved in working on it. If, in the pursuit of reducing a user's burden by 5%, you introduce 50% more complexity in its development, is the trade-off worthwhile?

- Maintain equilibrium in complexity. Deliberately determine the extent to which complexity is transferred between users and developers.

- Prior to streamlining processes, conduct an in-depth analysis to ascertain the necessity of such a feature.

Conclusion

Complexity cannot be generated or eliminated; it is merely shifted elsewhere. Every product comes with an inherent amount of irreducible complexity, and that cannot be just removed; the only question to be answered is, *who is going to deal with it, the designer, developer, or the user?*

As designers, we must shift most of the complexity from users to the system. In other words, we designers should deal with most of the complexity and let users deal with as little as possible. That is going to be the best product solution if the user is dealing with the least possible complexity.

However, in some scenarios, you should take a precautionary call before you simplify the complexity because, for a few products, the complexity adds flavor. It challenges the users to be more engaged, for example, in the games. Players play the games because it challenges them to participate and win. Another example is Photoshop, editors love to use this complex product because they can achieve extraordinary results after using these complex software options.

As per Tesler's law, we must transfer most of the complexity from users to the system but be cautious while doing so because a small portion of the complexity is loved by users.

In this chapter, we discussed handling and shifting complexity.

In the next chapter, we are going to discuss one of the most famous laws of psychology that is being used by most designers while designing layouts. We will discuss Gestalt law, the law of proximity.

Join our book's Discord space

Join the book's Discord Workspace for Latest updates, Offers, Tech happenings around the world, New Release and Sessions with the Authors:

https://discord.bpbonline.com

CHAPTER 6
Gestalt's Law

"Proximity, similarity, continuity and a few more rules, help the brain build patterns for easy information consumption."

Introduction

The human brain is a remarkably intricate organ with the ability to process vast amounts of information in nanoseconds. It is naturally inclined to recognize structure, logic, and patterns, aiding us in comprehending the complexities of the world.

In the 1920s, a cohort of German psychologists formulated theories known as Gestalt principles to explain how individuals perceive and interpret their surroundings. A collection of theories that delve into human perception—how our brains interpret visual information. Since the early 20th century, these principles have significantly shaped the design industry, leaving an indelible mark on numerous modern and iconic designs.

The Gestalt theory asserts that when confronted with a complex image or design comprising numerous elements, our brains naturally strive to formulate a form, pattern, or structure. The Gestalt principles represent the innate, subconscious shortcuts our brains employ to derive meaning from our surroundings.

These principles prove highly valuable for designers, serving as essential tools that enable them to communicate more information in a shorter time frame than would be achievable otherwise.

A key objective of design is problem-solving. Gestalt principles serve as valuable tools for designers by bringing order to chaos, allowing them to focus on crucial elements, and effectively conveying a wealth of information without overwhelming the audience with too much at once.

Structure

In this chapter, we are going to discuss a few principles that help the human mind build patterns while consuming information. With the help of these principles, the human mind finds the relativity between these objects, and with the help of building relationships between objects, the brain groups that information, making it easy to consume as well as memorize. One of the most important parts of a designer's job is designing a layout (pages, screens, and print material). This chapter covers the following topics:

- History
- Law of proximity
- Law of similarity
- Law of continuity
- Law of closure
- Law of focal point

Objectives

Gestalt Law has a lot of principles. We will discuss a few of the most used ones in this chapter. After understanding those principles, you will be able to do justice while arranging the information in your design, page, or screen. You will be able to define the priority of information for your users who need to consume it, and it is going to make their lives easier for sure by consuming more detailed information in less time.

History

The Gestalt Law was formulated during the 1920s by German psychologists *Max Wertheimer, Kurt Koffka,* and *Wolfgang Kohler.* The Gestalt principles made their debut in *Wertheimer's* works in 1923 and 1938. *Köhler* further expanded on these principles in 1929, while *Koffka* contributed in 1935.

The inception of the Gestalt's principles aimed to unravel the ways in which individuals comprehend and make sense of intricate visual and auditory stimuli. These principles specifically address the inherent tendency to impose order on disorder.

Originating in Austria and Germany, the Gestalt's theory emerged in response to the atomistic perspectives of associationist and structural schools. Gestalt studies embraced phenomenology as an alternative approach.

Their objective was to decipher how individuals make sense of the bewildering stimuli they encounter, both visually and aurally. Identifying a set of principles, they addressed the inherent inclination to impose order on chaos. According to these principles, the mind amalgamates individual elements into a cohesive whole, shaping perception.

The designers quickly embraced Gestalt's principles, using them to create eye-catching designs with well-placed elements.

The whole is other than the sum of the parts.

—Kurt Koffka

Let us start with the principles of the Gestalt's law:

- Law of proximity
- Law of similarity
- Law of continuity
- Law of closure
- Law of focal point

Law of proximity

The principle of proximity, within Gestalt psychology, elucidates how the human eye interprets elements in close proximity as more interconnected than those positioned farther apart. This rule holds true even when the elements exhibit variations in color, shape, size, or other distinctive characteristics.

This law helps you identify the group of information when you look at a big chunk of information. By creating appropriate spacing between these elements, our minds can discern patterns more easily and prioritize the flow of information for enhanced comprehension. If you notice *Figure 6.1*, you will notice those three groups of circles, although the color of all the circles are the same, which is green. It is all because of how the circles are arranged in terms of spacing between them:

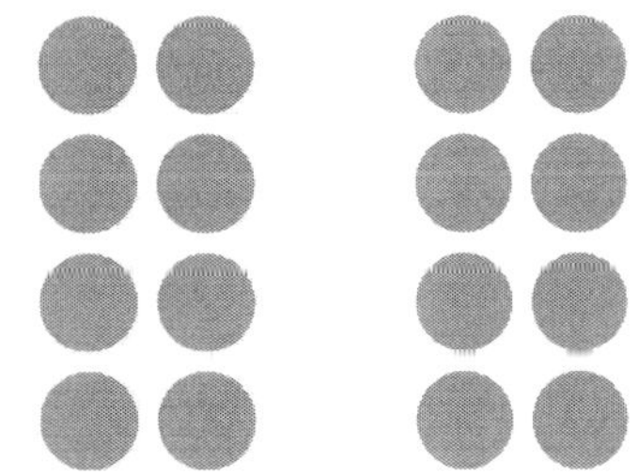

Figure 6.1: *Law of proximity: Example of with the Color*

The law of proximity is so strong that it overrides the quality of colors, shapes, and sizes. Now, if you notice *Figure 6.2*, you see there are two different-colored circles, but you can still notice three kinds of groups:

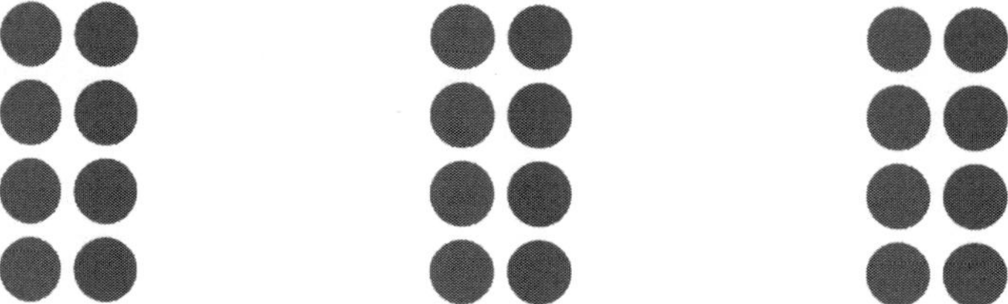

Figure 6.2: Law of proximity: Example with different colors

In this example, you will notice how the law of proximity overrides the color of the object. Our minds make a group of objects that are mixed in color. We group them into three groups because of how these circles are arranged in terms of the distance between them. This law is often used when designing a layout, page, or screen of an app where information is arranged. Let us look at a live example of how we may use this while designing the layout. In the following example, *Figure 6.3*, you will notice how the apparel pictures are aligned with the details so that our minds can easily create multiple groups to arrange the information in consumable format:

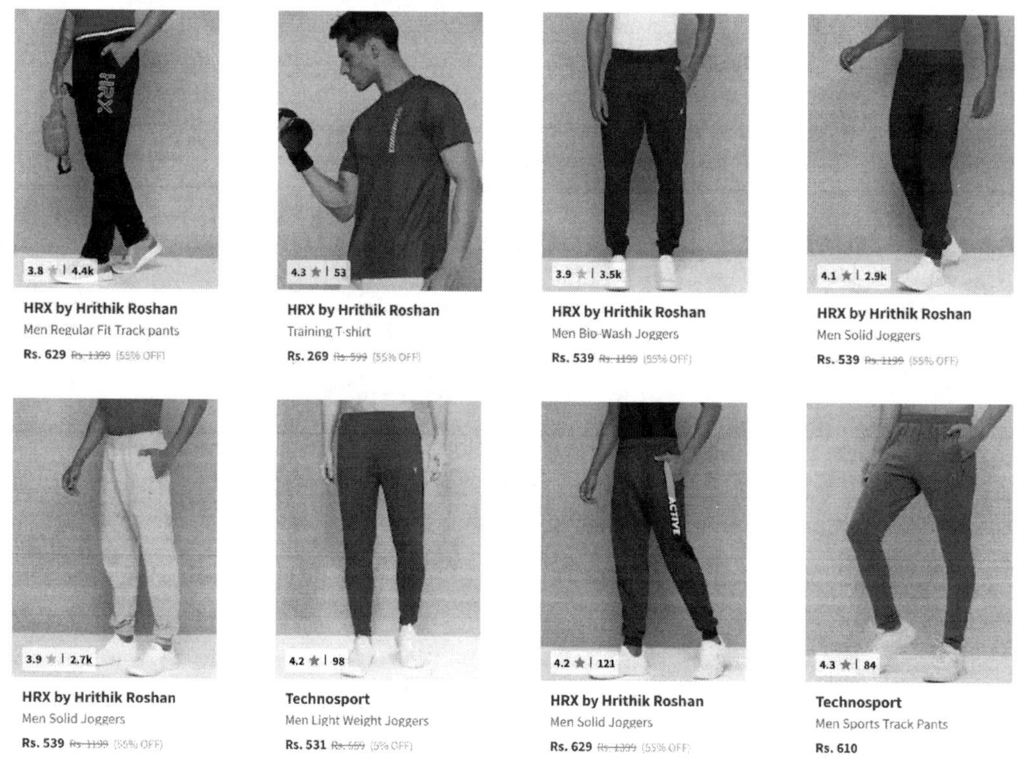

Figure 6.3: Law of Proximity: Example with LIVE Layouts

Law of similarity

The principle of similarity states that when things appear to be similar to each other, we group them together. Moreover, we also tend to think they have the same function (refer to the following figure):

Figure 6.4: Law of Similarity: Example with different shapes

A variety of design elements, like color and organization, can be used to establish similar groups. In *Figure 6.5*, for example, even though all the shapes are the same, each column represents a distinct group.

Figure 6.5: Law of similarity: Example with same shapes and different Colors

This law is also used a lot when you are designing a layout, page, or screen of an app where you arrange the information. Also, this law is being used a lot in a lot of board games, puzzle games, and toys for small kids to teach them similarity and relativity between the objects. Let us look at a live example of how we may use this while using it in LIVE projects.

If you notice *Figure 6.6*, you will see the similarity between the boxes (cards). It has one picture/image and two lines below it, and it is inside a container. Although the content of the boxes is different, the text and image are all different. But just because of the way it is arranged in all the boxes, they look similar, and our minds make the group accordingly.

Again, this trick must be used in designing the layout to showcase the groups. It makes it easy to relate to similar components and visualize those as a group.

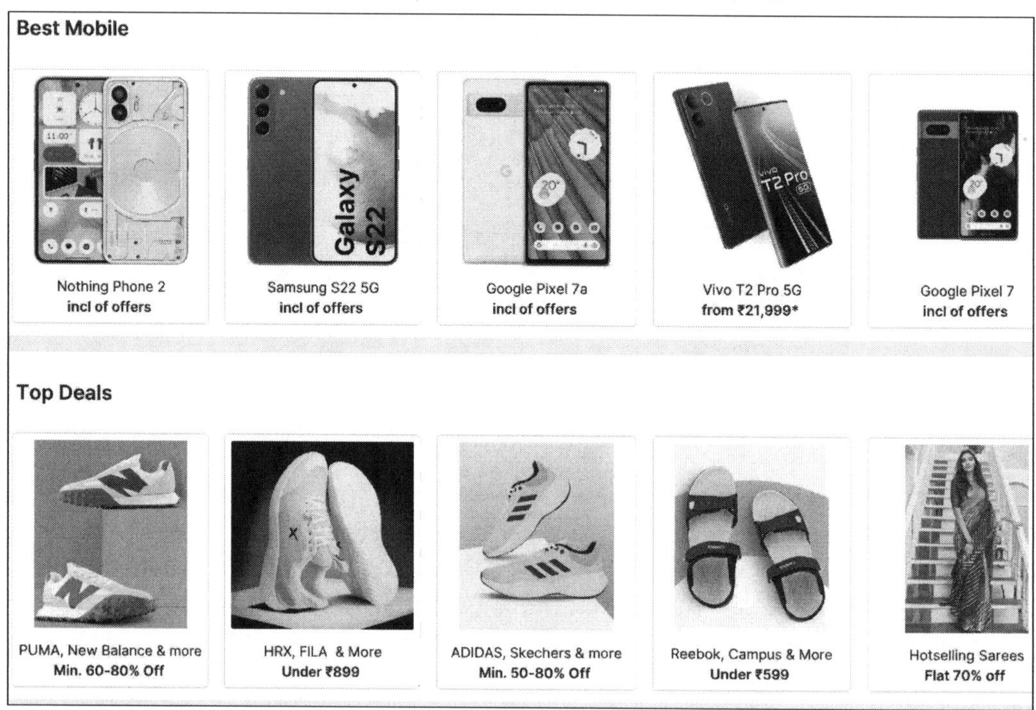

Figure 6.6: Law of Similarity: Example with LIVE Layouts

Law of continuity

The continuity principle asserts that elements positioned along a line or curve are perceived as more interconnected than those not situated on the line or curve.

When you notice *Figure 6.7*, you will observe two curves meeting at one center point. You will not see four curves meeting at a center point. Although you will not see any difference in color or shape, our mind understands this as two curves because of the continuity of the two curves.

It proves that when objects are arranged in a particular curve or line, they are one group because of continuity.

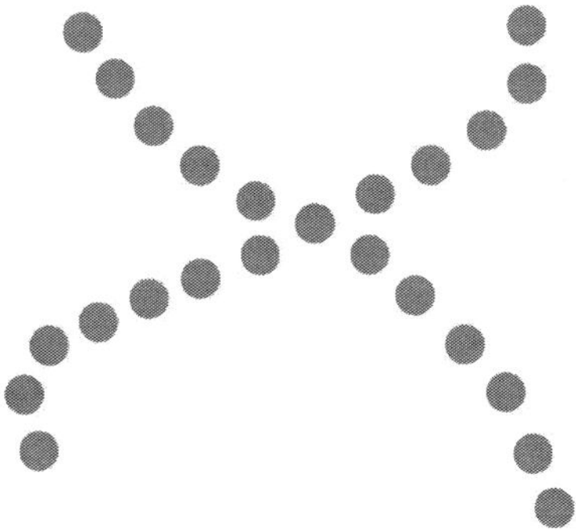

Figure 6.7: Law of continuity: Example of two curves

Now let us have a look at Pinterest's home feed interface in *Figure 6.8* as an example. Despite varying image sizes on the screen, they are organized in columns, forming seamless vertical lines of negative space between each picture. In this context, the continuity principle guides users to scroll vertically through the app, as the columnar layout promotes upward and downward movement.

Figure 6.8: Law of continuity: Pinterest feed example

Law of closure

The closure principle asserts that, despite missing parts in an image, the brain has the ability to fill in the gaps, allowing for the perception of a complete picture. For instance, in the illustration below, the circle and rectangle remain perceptible, even though the lines are fragmented.

If you notice *Figure 6.9*, the first shape your mind observes is a circle, and the second one is a square. But the reality is that it is neither a circle nor a square. Our mind fills the missing part with the closure principle and recognizes these as complete shapes.

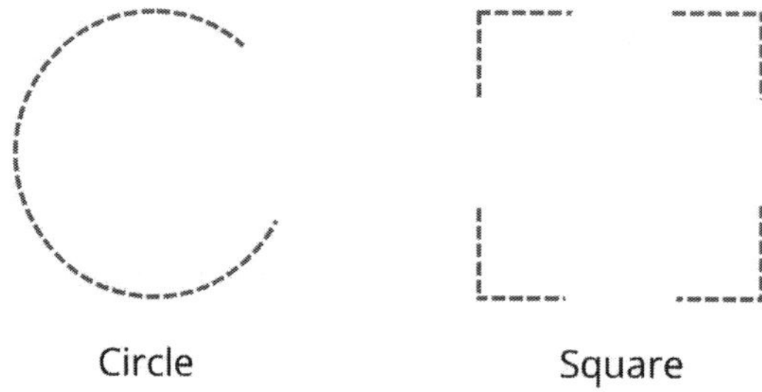

Figure 6.9: Law of Closure - incomplete shapes that looks complete

This rule is used in graphic design and some layout designs and is also seen as a gamification pattern to get the task completed by the users because users seem to fill in the gaps and complete a task that looks incomplete. For now, let us look at examples of how this rule helps in graphic design.

Look at the examples in *Figure 6.10* and *Figure 6.11*. You will see that the shapes in the IBM logo and other logos are not complete, but our mind still fills the gap and makes sense of those incomplete objects.

Figure 6.10: Law of closure: IBM Logo

Figure 6.11: Law of Closure: Logos with closure examples

Law of focal point

The principle of focal point declares that anything that visually stands out will seize and retain the viewer's attention initially.

Notice *Figure 6.12*, where there are 34 grey circles, but the maximum attention is paid to a red star because it stands out visually:

Figure 6.12: *Law of Focal point: Visually standing out object gets maximum attention*

The majority of designs incorporate focal points to guide the viewer's gaze toward a crucial element or encourage them to undertake a specific action. For instance, call-to-action buttons often feature contrasting colors for emphasis.

Similarly, this law is used a lot to attract the attention of the users to particular information or to focus on a particular action. For example, have a look at *Figure 6.13* and notice the focal point, which is the Buy Now button in red. Because of the focal point, attention goes to the red button, and it is very likely that the user will click this button. In the below figure, the focal point is used for the center plan, which is not the most cost-effective and does not have all the features, but the website chose to recommend a plan that is highly likely to be sold, so they used the focal point to highlight and grab the attention of the user so that the decision-making is quicker.

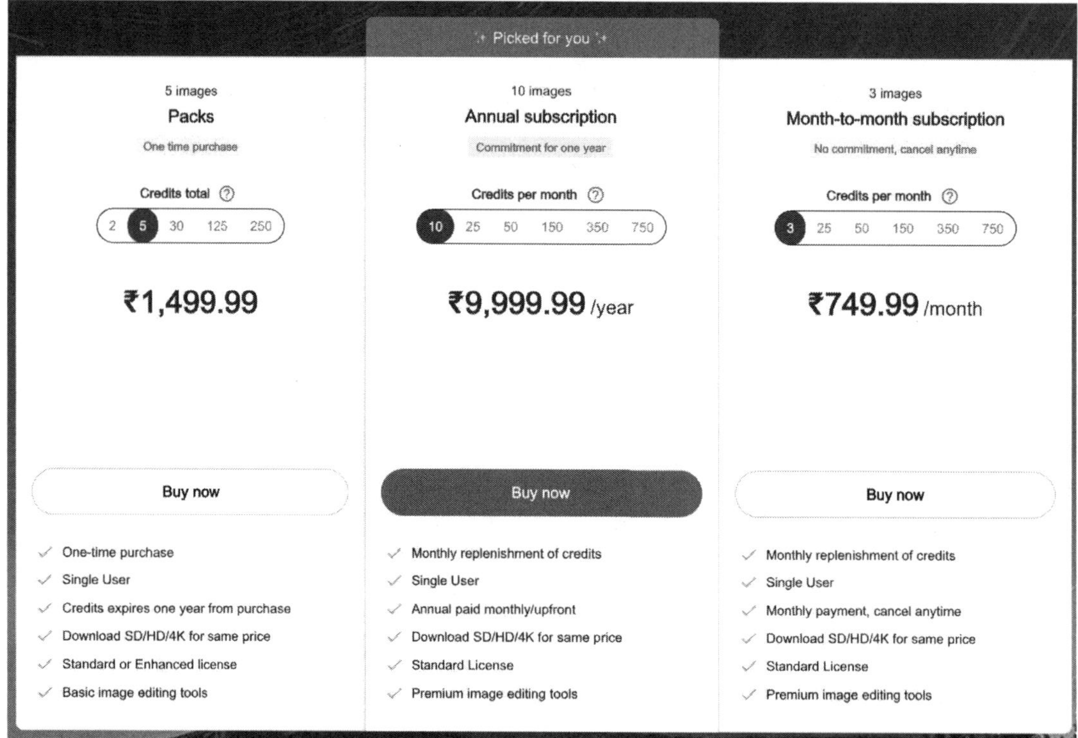

Figure 6.13: *Law of Focal point - Example of a focal point being on CTA (Button)*

Conclusion

There are multiple Gestalt principles that help the designers plan the layout in such a manner that it becomes easy for the users to consume the information. We discussed a few out of so many, which are the laws of proximity, similarity, continuity, closure, and focal point. Other than these, there are a few more that you should explore yourself, like figure-ground, common region, uniform connectedness, common fate, parallelism, experience, and so on.

Till now, we have discussed a few laws of psychology. Now, in the coming chapters, we are going to discuss a few effects that psychologically affect our decision-making, both for design and for other stuff. We are going to start with the Doherty threshold.

CHAPTER 7

Doherty Threshold

"Users get disinterested after 400 ms inactivity."

Introduction

The principle of Doherty Threshold states that a computer or a product should respond to a user's action within 400 milliseconds. This ensures the user does not feel like they are waiting for a response. The Doherty Threshold is named after the researcher who first described it.

The Doherty Threshold is a key principle for effective UX design. It states that productivity increases when a computer and its users interact at a pace of less than 400 ms.

Structure

In this chapter, we are going to discuss the Doherty Threshold, which tells about the value of time. How do users get disinterested in your product / computer if it does not respond for 400 ms. We will discuss about:

- History of Doherty Threshold
- Real life examples of Doherty Threshold and how to use it

Objectives

Your understanding of Doherty Threshold is going to make or break your system. It is a very important trick to learn for user acquisition and retention. Remember that users are always impatient, and they want their tasks to be completed as soon as possible. With the help of timely feedback, we may create a good experience for the users. In this chapter, we will discuss how to use this effect diligently to design a good user flow.

History

In 1982, *Walter J. Doherty* and *Ahrvind J. Thadani* presented a research paper in the IBM Systems Journal, establishing a new standard for computer response time at 400 milliseconds. This marked a departure from the previous standard of 2,000 milliseconds (2 seconds). If a computer executed and returned a response to a human command within 400 milliseconds, it was considered to surpass the *Doherty Threshold*, and applications with such responsiveness were classified as potentially *addicting* to users.

Let us think of a scenario where you try ordering food online via an app or website from your mobile device. You thought of having a lamb burger today, and you searched for a lamb burger in the search bar. After you tap the search button, your screen turns blank, and it seems something will load. Now the question is:

- What is going to be your next step? Of course, you will wait because you are hungry.
- But the question is how much time will you wait for a web page / mobile screen to load? 2 seconds, 4 seconds or 10 seconds?

As per the research by *Walter J. Doherty* and *Ahrvind J*, a user starts losing interest after just 400 ms. In that case, expecting a user to wait for 2, 4, or 10 seconds is too much of an expectation.

The probability is so high that you will either try to reload the page or leave the platform and move to another platform to fulfill your need for ordering food.

Here, the key learnings for the designers are as follows:

- Do not let your users wait for more than 400 ms in any user journey.
- If the system is taking more than 400 milliseconds, then engage the users.
- More than engaging them, it is important to pass on the feedback to the users that we are working on your request and how much time is expected to let users reach the next goal or inform them honestly about the current status. You know, as we have all learned since childhood, honesty is the best policy.

Examples of Doherty Threshold

Now, let us explore some examples that demonstrate the correct way to update users about progress.

I am sure you must have seen such loaders in your user journey on multiple platforms. Refer to *Figure 7.1*:

Figure 7.1: Loading screen with text written and animating or circular animation

When you are waiting for feedback from the system, the loaders above assure you that the system is working, and we must have some patience as a user. At least users have some assurance that something is cooking, but to what extent is it correct to have such a loader? Imagine you have this loader running for 7-10 seconds; does this solve the purpose? Will the user still be interested and wait on your screen for you to load the next screen? I assume no. It is not the right way to engage the user if you are going to take a lot of time.

This time of loader is good to have when you have a very minor waiting time, which could be up to 1-2 seconds, not more than that.

So now the question is, what to do if the waiting time is more than 1-2 seconds? It could be a system requirement, or sometimes your users might be in a compromised network condition, and the waiting time could be more than 1-2 seconds.

Let us look at *Figure 7.2* that fits this scenario.

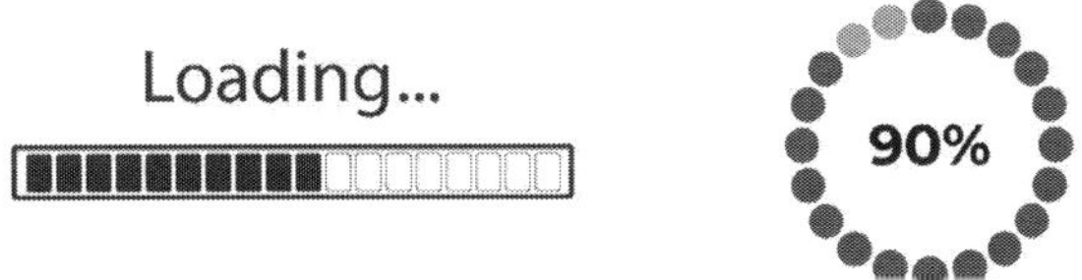

Figure 7.2: Loading screen with progress information

In this example, users are informed about the current status of the process so that they are well aware of the time he/she should wait.

In the first one, it is visually communicated that it is almost half done and waiting for this much time to get to the next screen, and in the second example of the circular loader with 90% done, it is communicated very clearly that only 10% more time is left to load the next screen.

Now, as per the *Doherty Threshold*, users will be disinterested after 400 ms. They will be well informed about the status and time needed to wait, or at least the user can take their call about how much time to wait. This process will also engage the users to stick and wait for an expected time.

This way of 'informing' the user is a better solution to deal with the *Doherty Threshold* effect. Few more common examples nowadays is that, in many apps when they inform the users about the current status via sharing specific progress. For example, let us focus on *Figure 7.3*.

Imagine that you are uploading images/pictures to a certain platform, and once you tap/click on upload, a loader like *Figure 7.3* appears and you observe the information on the loader is quite useful because:

- It shows how much of the process is done.

- Percentage gives a clear idea of how much more time is needed to complete the task.

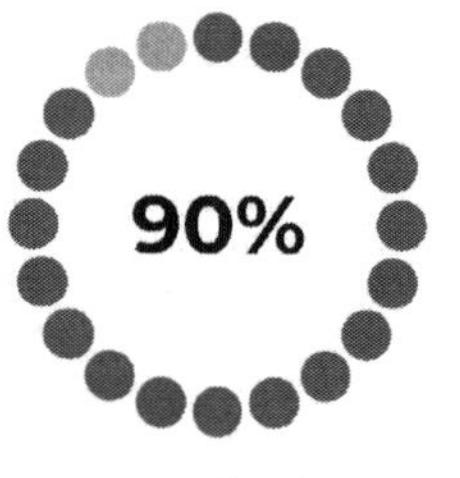

Figure 7.3: Loading screen with specific progress information

- On top of percentage information, it also gives specific information about the current task being done, like in the example it says - *compressing images*. It gives one a level of extra clarity, that for the images being uploaded, the system is compressing first, before it starts uploading, and I will get to know when the system starts uploading and also when it is done.

With the help of the above examples of handling the Doherty Threshold, you will be able to make your user wait for more than 400 ms. We need to be aware of when we should use what kind of solution.

Now, there is another way to look at this problem statement. Till now, we have been focusing on how to engage the users, give feedback, and inform them about the status so that they stay or wait for more than 400 ms.

Let us understand what happens when a user gets a response within 400 ms:

According to Doherty's Threshold, the transition from a challenging user experience to an addictive one occurs when the system feedback time falls below 400 milliseconds.

Few achieve this via quick feedback, faster response, a loader screen, or engaged animation. We discussed the types of loaders to be used in different scenarios. However, if we want to have a loader or some other animation to engage the users, what should be the right duration of the animation? If you are looking for a specific number/duration of the animation, here is something to ponder about:

Should you prefer to substitute Doherty's Threshold with specific numerical values, consider the following: Our brains complete the processing of images in 100 milliseconds, with an average response time of 250 milliseconds. According to Google's Material Design guidelines, basic animations should ideally conclude in 100 milliseconds, while more intricate ones may extend to 500 milliseconds.

Now, the animation need not be just the screen transition. A user expects feedback on every action, which could be as small as liking a status on social media. Just think about what happens when you tap on it; for example, when you like, the icon and text color change. You see a micro-interaction that feels like you tapped the button, and maybe there is some sound as well.

For example, refer to *Figure 7.4*. It is a LinkedIn social media post on which a user can take action below it, that is, - Like, comment, repost, and send to someone.

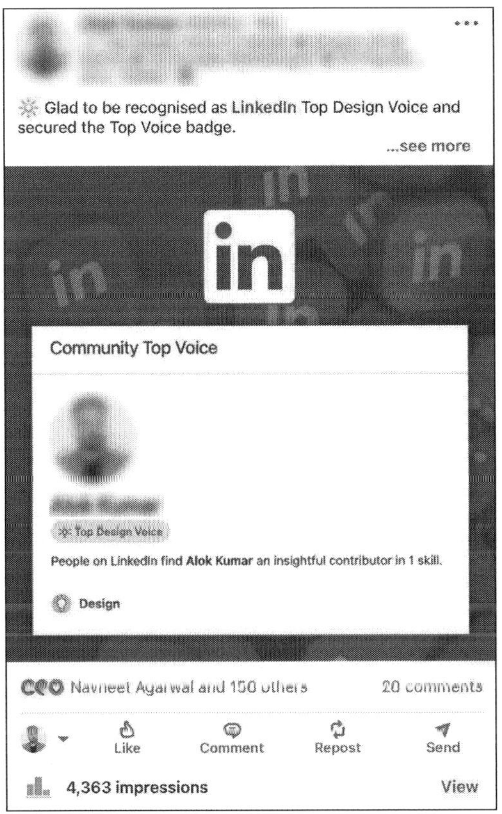

Figure 7.4: Social media post, before feedback

For example, when you long-press on the like icon or link, a top section appears very suddenly with these six types of expressions (refer to *Figure 7.5*). This animation shows the expression options, and it gives me immediate feedback that I must choose one of them to show my expression.

Figure 7.5: Social media post, feedback options / interaction

In the moment if one chooses any, it changes the status from Like to love with these icons highlighted as if they are active buttons, (refer to *Figure 7.6*), I immediately got feedback on my action. I know I tried to like it, and I chose my expression, which got applied, and my task is complete. This happens in a fraction of a second. That is the beauty of the Doherty Threshold.

Figure 7.6*: Social media post - after feedback*

Sometimes, when you get this experience, you do not even remember, but the reality is that you get habituated and addicted to such an experience. Sometimes, when you lack this experience, you tend to feel annoyed. If the feedback is given within 400 ms, your action turns into a good experience, and that experience leads to addiction.

Now, let us talk about another addiction that most individuals in this world are addicted to. Do you watch reels on Instagram or shorts on YouTube? Do you realize that you might have started to watch one of the shorts on your mobile device, but you end up watching so many, that you just do not realize how many you have seen while swiping and moving to the next one. Refer to the following figure:

Figure 7.7: Students enjoying watching short videos on mobile

Have you ever realized why it happens? One of the biggest reasons is that you are watching something that you like, and these platforms personalize your videos/experiences as per your likes and viewing patterns. But have you ever thought about the videos on certain topics that you loved (inspirational, funny, informative, etc.) were always there on YouTube and some other platforms, but the question is that were you watching those earlier as well with similar frequency? It may be that you were not that addicted earlier, but now you are addicted.

One of the reasons for this is the Doherty Threshold; you can switch to the next video quickly by swiping up or left. The duration of these videos is really short (below 1 minute). Users were given feedback and the action within seconds. Before you take a call on what you should see next video, the next video is already on your screen, and you are actually already watching it because of the speed at which it appears.

Since you take the next action within 400 ms, you seem to be engaged and very interested, and that engagement turns into an addiction. It has been that long now that the whole world is busy consuming video information of their own choice with just one swipe.

Let us look at another few examples how Doherty Threshold is employed at multiple platform in your buying journey (e-commerce, food ordering, etc.)

Ever noticed the **Buy Now** button on Amazon other than **Add to Cart**? Ever thought about why Amazon has both buttons on each product page? Refer to *Figure 7.8* of Amazon's product detail page with the **Add to Cart** and **Buy Now** buttons:

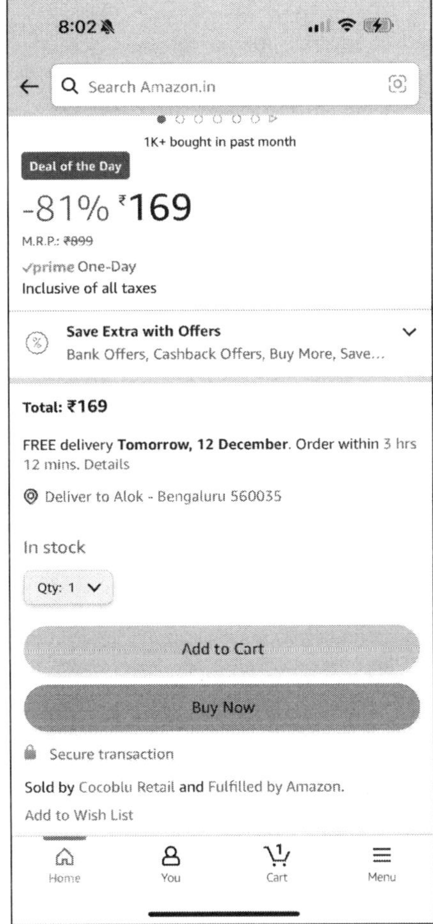

Figure 7.8: Amazon's Buy Now (Quick Buy) feature

The 1-Click ordering functionality on Amazon also utilizes the Doherty Threshold. Upon selecting the **Buy Now with 1-Click** button, the order undergoes immediate processing, ensuring a rapid and seamless shopping experience. You do not need to go to the cart or check the address, they provide this information on a small half card. Proceed to the final payment page, and you are done before you change your mind.

Another example is Swiggy's single-page checkout flow. Refer to *Figure 7.9*, Swiggy's **Cart**. After adding your food items in the cart, you get the option to swipe and checkout. It is an advanced attempt at technology by providing a swipe-to-pay option, but it also employs the Doherty Threshold very well. Similarly, it selects your last payment mode/preferred payment mode by default and gives you the option to swipe and pay. So that user does not go to the multiple payment mode and selects and spends some time there. By providing a quick checkout option, users tend to skip the rest of the steps and quickly choose their option. It reacts as quickly as possible. Please refer to the following figure:

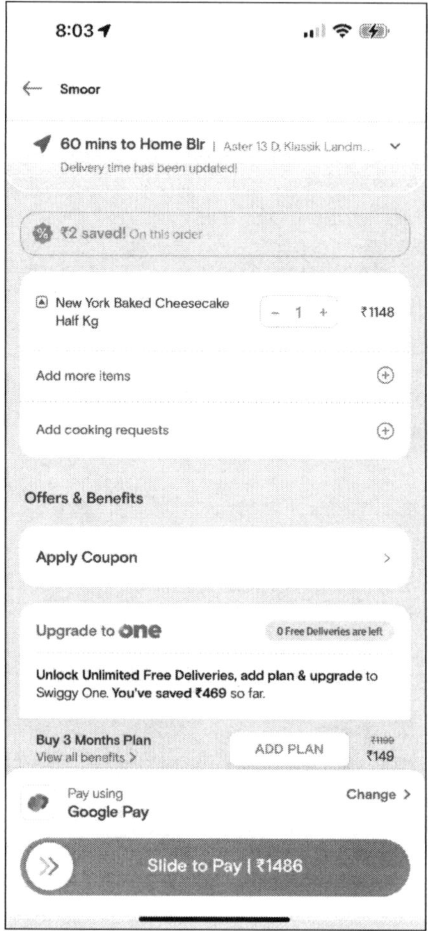

Figure 7.9: *Swiggy's quick checkout with one swipe feature*

This effect is used to motivate users to be focused and take certain actions quickly, which leads to a good conversion.

We discussed a few live examples of the Doherty Threshold and understood how it is used in the live products to make the user experience wow for the users.

Conclusion

The Doherty Threshold is a trick that every product designer must know and use if you are willing to engage your users and bring their attention to your product/feature. By giving feedback within 400 ms, you may grab the complete interest of your users in your product, and we all know that engagement and retention are target metrics that most designers are chasing.

Use this effect cautiously to give your users the best experience. In a few live examples, we saw quick feedback on action items with micro-interactions and skipped the extra steps to complete the task quickly, like quick checkout and single-page checkout.

We hope you learned and will use this effect in your product interactions. In the next chapter, we are going to deep dive into another effect of psychology, i.e., the Zeigarnik effects which tell us about the user's behavior around a complete and incomplete task. This effect is slightly influenced by the Closure behavior of Gestalt law. We will discuss how incomplete tasks influence the user's ability to complete them and how designers can use this effect to get the tasks completed by the users.

Join our book's Discord space

Join the book's Discord Workspace for Latest updates, Offers, Tech happenings around the world, New Release and Sessions with the Authors:

https://discord.bpbonline.com

Section II
Psychological Effects

Psychological effects play a crucial role in design by influencing how users perceive, interact with, and respond to a product or environment. Leveraging these effects can greatly enhance the effectiveness, appeal, and usability of a design. Here are few psychological effects in design that will help:

CHAPTER 8
Zeigarnik Effect

"People remember incomplete tasks better than completed ones."

Introduction

Commencing a task but leaving it incomplete often leads to persistent thoughts about the unfinished work, even as you engage in other activities. These lingering thoughts compel you to revisit and complete the task you initiated. This phenomenon explains why your mind keeps returning to that captivating book or motivates you to continue playing a video game until you achieve victory. The impact of unfinished work persists, subtly influencing our focus even when we attempt to shift our attention to different pursuits.

In this chapter, we are going to discuss the Zeigarnik effects. An effect that reminds you all the time of your incomplete tasks, and you tend to think about finishing those. In the design industry, it can influence users to complete a task. We will learn about the origin and reason for this effect, how to use it in designing the experience to drive user motivation, and how it is being used in live products.

Structure

In this chapter, we will discuss the following topics:

- History
- Use cases of the Zeigarnik effect
- Tips to use Zeigarnik effect

Objectives

Your understanding of Zeigarnik effects will help you understand this effect deeply, and you will be able to relate how to use this effect to positively impact your product and influence user behavior by certainly using this effect. Also, we will learn about how it is being used in live products.

History

The Zeigarnik effect, named after its founder, Russian psychiatrist, and psychologist *Bluma Wulfovna Zeigarnik*, originated from her observations in a 1920s restaurant. While noting that waiters efficiently managed complex orders and unpaid bills, their ability to recall details diminished once orders were filled and paid for. Intrigued by this phenomenon, *Zeigarnik* conducted experiments in her laboratory to understand it better.

Zeigarnik assigned 138 children simple tasks, puzzles, and arithmetic problems in one experiment. The children completed half of the tasks, while interruptions occurred during the remaining ones. After an hour's delay, *Zeigarnik* examined their recall and found that 110 out of 138 children demonstrated better memory for the interrupted tasks than those they completed. A parallel experiment involving adults revealed that participants could recall unfinished tasks 90% more effectively than completed ones.

As per Zeigarnik, When you begin working towards an objective and do not achieve it, your mind will frequently remind you of that goal while engaging in other activities, nudging you to resume your efforts and complete what you started.

The Zeigarnik effect is a psychological phenomenon that refers to people's better memory of uncompleted or interrupted tasks than completed ones. Even if you are busy with some other work, your incomplete work is always going on in your subconscious mind because it is the effect of the Zeigarnik effect.

Now, since this is a psychological theory, it is happening to most of us, and this can be used in many digital products to motivate users to complete a task. This can be an excellent asset for designers and product managers looking to retain and engage their users. This trick can motivate users to complete an incomplete task with a simple nudge.

In the previous chapter, Gesalt's law of closure that refers to incomplete things that our mind relates to a complete thing.

Refer to the following figure:

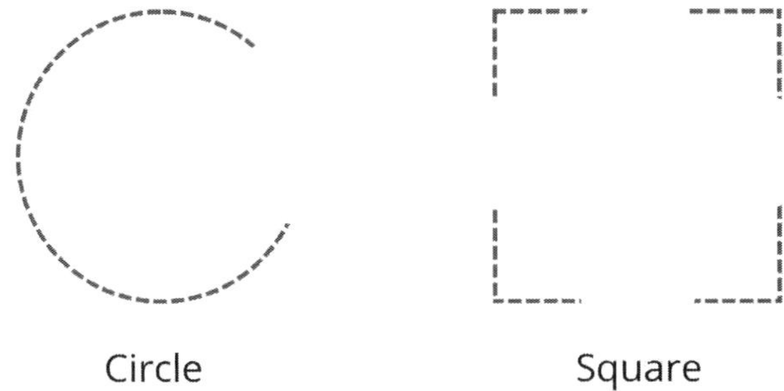

Figure 8.1: *Law of closure - shapes that look complete*

If you notice *Figure 8.1*, the first shape your mind observes is a circle, and the second is a square. However, the reality is that it is neither a circle nor a square. Our mind fills the missing part with the closure principle and recognizes these as complete shapes.

The law of closure and the Zeigarnik effect are a bit related. The reality is that when our mind looks at or imagines an incomplete task, it always prompts us to think about it, and we end up trying to complete it or completing it.

Let us look at a few examples where the Zeigarnik effect is being used to motivate users to complete a task.

Many platforms motivate you to complete your profile so that they have enough information to personalize your experience to a more significant extent. For example, LinkedIn, Naukri, and a few more platforms show your profile as partially completed (*Figure 8.2*) when you log in. When you see your profile at 25% or 70% complete, you finish it as soon as possible because that is going through your mind:

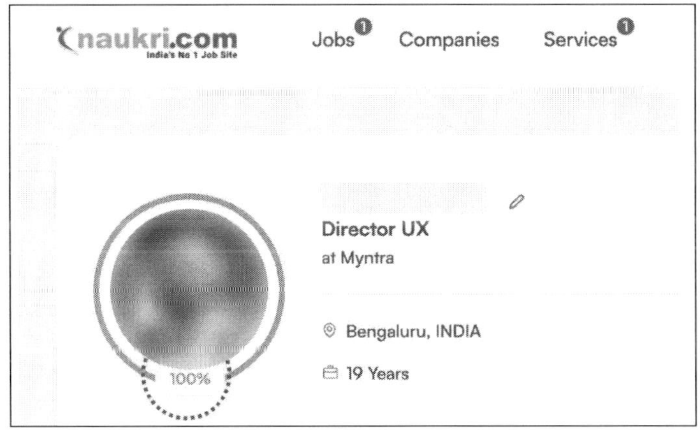

Figure 8.2: *Naukri Profile completion: 100%*

These platforms never show you that your profile is 0% complete, whether you have put your name and some information. When a user sees 0% complete, they feel they need to start a task, whereas when a user sees it is partially done, they are encouraged to put in the effort and complete their profile. That is the power of the Zegarnik effect, but it should be used wisely. The following figure shows partial development:

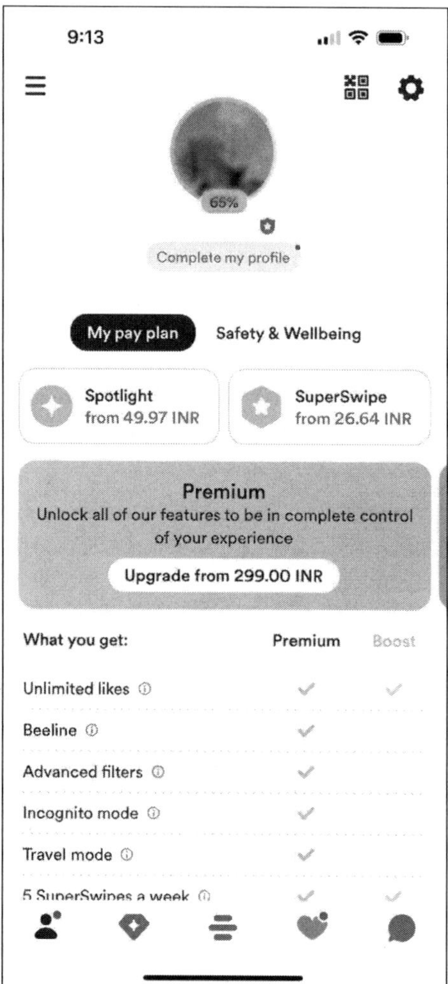

Figure 8.3*: Bumble profile completion*

Refer to the following figure:

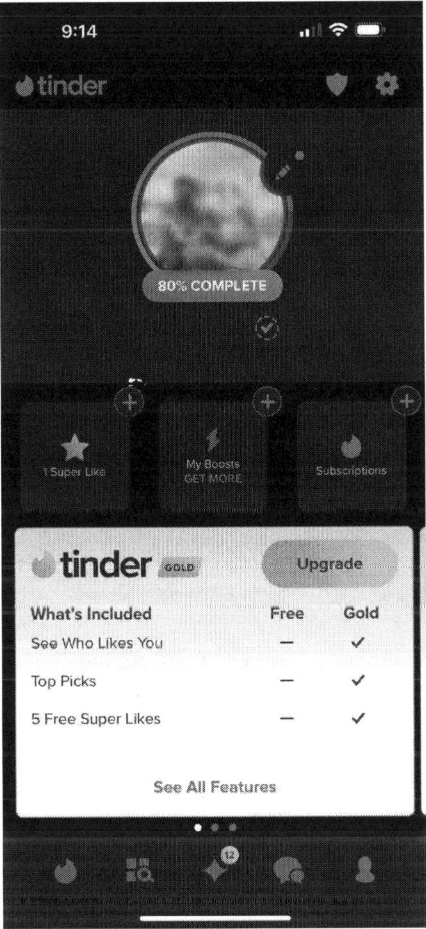

Figure 8.4: Tinder profile completion

Do not negatively reinforce your users by informing them that your progress is zero. For example, consider *Figure 8.3* and *Figure 8.4*. Even after putting minimal information in Bumble and Tinder, it shows the profile completion as a good number, reinforcing the desire to complete it. Also, these platforms can upsell their other products, like membership and upgrade plans, to get better business, and users tend to avail themselves of those.

Now, let us look at *Figure 8.5*, which is from one of the famous mobile games, Royal Clash. Usually, gamers play the game to entertain themselves, make some records, and collect some exclusive badges to brag about with their social friends:

Figure 8.5: Royal Clash game: My badges

If you notice, in the Badges section, it shows us that we got only one badge, but showcasing space for seven more badges reinforces that we should play more and achieve more badges so that we can brag about our entire house of badges to our friends.

Empty badges fill places, and having one badge gives us the Zeigarnik effect that always hits our minds. We have to achieve seven more badges to fill our badge box.

To manage the influx of information, individuals often employ cognitive strategies to enhance memory retention. The Zeigarnik effect illustrates one such technique, wherein we repeatedly bring uncompleted tasks to mind, maintaining them in our short-term memory. This frequent mental review helps us remember these tasks more effectively until we can see them through to completion.

The Zeigarnik effect suggests that not only do incomplete tasks linger in our short-term memory, but they can also frequently resurface in our thoughts over a long time. This phenomenon shows the information journey from sensory memory to long-term storage, with attention and active rehearsal critical to this transition. Zeigarnik theorized that an incomplete task generates cognitive tension, prompting more mental effort to keep it in our awareness, which is relieved once the task is finished.

Besides digital products, the Zeigarnik effect also helps with daily real-life examples.

Use cases of the Zeigarnik effect

Here are a few steps that may impact that will help the user:

- **Tackle procrastination**: This psychological phenomenon is particularly effective for mitigating procrastination. Often, we delay significant tasks due to their daunting nature. The Zeigarnik effect proposes that initiating the task, even with a minor step, is crucial. Ideally, this initial step should be straightforward, creating an unfinished task that consumes our mental energy. This incomplete state triggers discomfort, prompting us to finalize the task freeing our minds from its constant presence.

Figure 8.6: *A student focusing on study*

A quick routine/steps for you could be:

o   Make a plan

o   Start with a small and manageable first step

o   Do not try to complete the task right away

Taking baby steps and being consistent will help you achieve the goal if you do not complete the smaller milestone immediately. That incomplete task will prompt you to complete it.

- **Enhancing study techniques**: For students preparing for exams, the Zeigarnik effect offers valuable insights. It suggests that segmenting study periods can boost memory retention. Rather than engaging in prolonged, uninterrupted study sessions, it is beneficial to incorporate breaks focusing on different activities.

These intervals induce recurring thoughts about the study material, aiding in its rehearsal and consolidation, ultimately enhancing recall during exams.

Figure 8.7: A student focusing on study

- **Influence your mental health**: The Zeigarnik effect also sheds light on the potential causes of mental health issues. Incomplete tasks can generate persistent intrusive thoughts, leading to stress, anxiety, sleep disturbances, and overall mental exhaustion. Conversely, this effect can positively impact mental health by motivating task completion. Finishing tasks, especially those that are stressful, not only provides a sense of accomplishment and boosts self-esteem but also brings a sense of closure, contributing to improved mental well-being.

Figure 8.8: People focusing on their mental health

The Zeigarnik effect also sheds light on the potential causes of mental health issues. Incomplete tasks can generate persistent intrusive thoughts, leading to stress, anxiety, sleep disturbances, and overall mental exhaustion. Conversely, this effect can positively impact mental health by motivating task completion. Finishing tasks, especially those that are stressful, that not only provides a sense of accomplishment and boosts self-esteem but also brings a sense of closure, contributing to an improved mental well-being.

Tips to use Zeigarnik effect

Since now we discussed the example and impact of the Zeigarnik effect, let us summarize few tips and tricks to use Zeigarnik effect impactfully:

- It is always easier to complete an incomplete task than to start a new one.
- Employ various design methods to grab users' focus and spark their interest in the task.
- Generate curiosity and highlight the benefits to persuade users to engage willingly.
- Strategically incorporate breaks to create cognitive tension, motivating users towards the product or service without causing frustration.
- Prompt users to finalize tasks by guiding them toward the end goal.

Conclusion

The Zeigarnik effect is an effect of psychology that is a bit connected to the law of closure of Gestalt law. This law shows the power of incomplete tasks; the recall value of an incomplete task is way higher than that of a complete one. This incompletion of a task keeps you from completing it. Since it is a psychological phenomenon, we as designers must implement this effect in our digital product solutions. This effect is used to motivate users to complete the partially completed task. It is usually seen that the ratio of completing the partially completed task is way higher than starting and completing a new task. We will use this effect in product interactions.

In the next chapter, we will dive deep into another significant part of the design and psychology world: storytelling. Storytelling is as important as developing a design. The story has to be impactful and meaningful. It should define the pitch and probability of the design or idea to be sold to the stakeholders. So, it is a must-learn art for every designer.

Join our book's Discord space

Join the book's Discord Workspace for Latest updates, Offers, Tech happenings around the world, New Release and Sessions with the Authors:

https://discord.bpbonline.com

CHAPTER 9

Storytelling Effect

"People remember stories better than facts alone."

— Walter J Lippmann

Introduction

Storytelling fosters empathy and trust between the narrator and the audience. By sharing personal experiences, values, and viewpoints through stories, the storyteller invites the audience to understand and see the world from their perspective. The storyteller has the power to influence and impact the listeners. Storytelling is a powerful tool that leaves a big impact on the human mind.

Structure

In this chapter, we are going to discuss the power and impact of storytelling with some examples, and we will discuss previous experiments around it. How can storytelling be used for the design we present to the stakeholders, and what are the few key points to be taken care of? Moreover, we will discuss some tips on Storytelling.

The topics we will discuss in this chapter are as follows:

- History
- Tips on how to use storytelling

Objectives

It is being observed that most of the early designers who are good at crafting interesting designs with a good visual sense but lack the skill to convince the stakeholders consequently get frustrated that their designs are being rejected or changed. People lack the skill of storytelling and the ability to convey the impactful reason behind the thought process they applied. We will discuss the value of Storytelling so that it will help the folks convey the message to the stakeholder.

History

Storytelling is a fundamental part of human culture, possibly emerging soon after language development. All cultures engage in storytelling, with ancient evidence found in cave drawings like those in *Lascaux* and *Chavaux*, France, dating back 30,000 years. These images potentially represent early visual stories. Oral storytelling, an age-old tradition transcending cultures, is storytelling through speech and gestures, encompassing various forms such as epic poems, chants, and songs. This tradition includes a wide range of narratives, from myths and fables to religious texts and proverbs.

> *Storytelling is a contextual bridge between play and written narrative.*
>
> — *Bruner, Saracho and Spadek*

At its core, a story depicts the dynamics of life's changes. It typically starts in a state of equilibrium—like a regular work routine. However, an unexpected event, or inciting incident, disrupts this balance. This could be a new job offer, a sudden loss, or a major client threat. The narrative then unfolds around the protagonist's struggle to reconcile their expectations with the harsh realities of life. Through this journey, the protagonist is forced to confront challenges, make tough decisions, and eventually confront the truth. This timeless theme of conflicting expectations and reality has been a cornerstone of storytelling, from ancient Greek tales to Shakespearean dramas and modern narratives.

From an early age, you might have been exposed to countless stories, from those your mother told you to the various books, movies, and plays you have experienced. Humans innately process experiences as narratives. Cognitive psychologists have found that the human mind naturally constructs stories from life's events, starting with personal ambitions and the challenges faced in achieving them. Our memories favor narratives over simple lists or bullet points, highlighting the power of storytelling in shaping our understanding and recollections.

In business, it is essential not only to comprehend the company's history but also to envisage its future, much like crafting a story. Business professionals imagine future possibilities for their companies or personal lives by creating mental scenarios. Recognizing that the human mind naturally frames experiences as narratives, successful business communication involves embracing this tendency and engaging audiences through compelling storytelling.

*By mastering the art of storytelling and unleashing your imagination, you can
captivate and energize an audience, leading to overwhelming applause
rather than disinterest and inattention*

— Maya Angelou

When I assess the requirement of storytelling in the world of UX design, I can say with conviction that there is a need for it. Designers do follow a lot of processes and do a lot of primary and secondary research.

For example, a graphic designer follows the given steps before finalizing a design:

- MoodBoard is a collage of inspirations, graphics, text, color, and so on
- Secondary research about the font style.
- Observe the colors of the industry / trends / competition, and so on.
- Plan some visual elements and illustrations.
- Decide the theme of illustrations and few more and then finally they execute the final design after few iterations

If we talk about UX designers, their processes to solve a UX problems are like:

- Primary / secondary research: Meeting users or researching on internet
- Competitive analysis – Checkout the competition and observe
- Data analysis of the current product / design to deep-dive the problem statement
- User journey mapping – Check how the user performs the task currently
- Brainstorming for solution – Look for multiple solution within a group of folks
- Task flow, information architecture – Plan the new and easier flow for the user
- Wireframe, visuals and many more – Work on final look and feel of the final design

However, when they have to present the designs to the stakeholders, they will end up showcasing the final designs and taking feedback on those. Everyone has an opinion on a design based on logic, subjectivity, or bias in their own mind. This is the place where storytelling plays an important role.

A designer needs to plan the story of making this design and showcase the complete process that led him/her to this output/solution. When you present your story with the processes, logic and thought that has gone behind it, the stakeholders will not hesitate to support it. If you use storytelling well, you will see its impact in your presentation as well as the outcomes.

Let me tell you a very interesting story about the power of Storytelling and how does it impact the user decision.

Let us look at an interesting example where the power of storytelling and how it impacts user decision is showcased. Have you ever heard of the *Significant Objects* project?

The **Significant Objects** project, created by *Rob Walker* and *Joshua Glenn*, was a unique literary and anthropological experiment. It proved that an object's perceived value can be objectively influenced by the stories attached to it.

Rob Walker and *Joshua Glenn* conducted an experiment to see if attaching personal narratives to inexpensive things (average cost $1.25) sold on eBay could significantly boost their value. Their theory was that emotionally rich stories would substantially raise each item's perceived worth, resulting in a considerable profit from their sales.

For their experiment, *Walker* and *Glenn* acquired approximately $129 of thrift store objects, such as a ceramic horse bust and a cow-shaped creamer. They then collaborated with over 200 writers to craft imaginative stories for these items, aiming to infuse them with sentimental value that would elevate their appeal beyond their ordinary nature.

Out of those multiple objects, there was a horse bust as well (refer to the following figure). For your reference, refer to *Figure 9.1*, which is not any extra-ordinary art. It was a decent art sculpture that was not very costly as well. And there was a good story written about this horse as well, with great sentimental value and entertaining side.

Figure 9.1: *The horse bust sold with a good story*

The horse bust, acquired for just $ 0.99, became the subject of an entertaining story created by an author. This narrative humorously revolved around her father's antics as a clumsy drunk in France during the 1970s, including a peculiar encounter with a horse.

The horse bust, initially bought for just $0.99, was sold for an impressive $62.95, marking a staggering 6258.58% increase in value. This trend was mirrored in the sale of other items, with the project cumulatively generating nearly $8,000 in revenue, showcasing a remarkable success.

So, what did we learn from this story?

Objects have less value without any story. Those were the same piece of art that was sold at a very high cost when an entertaining story was attached to it. People perceived the objects as they were told in the story thus increasing the value of art as well. The object on the other hand was easy to sell with an impactful price as well.

Storytelling also changes the perception of the listener. A similar stuff or story may impact differently to different personalities, and everyone may have their own version of the story as per their perception or cultural bias.

In 1944, in a study, psychologists *Fritz Heider* and *Marianne Simmel* asked participants to watch a brief animated film and subsequently narrate the events they observed.

The animated film contains 3 shapes: a small triangle, one big triangle, and one circle. All these shapes were moving with different speeds, motions, and directions. This was an almost minute-long animated movie that has been seen by thousands now and everyone had their own story and learnings when they are asked to describe this 1-minute animated movie. You may easily find this animated film on YouTube when you search for *Heider* and *Simmel* animation 1944 SD. (Link for experimental video: **http://surl.li/tlhox**)

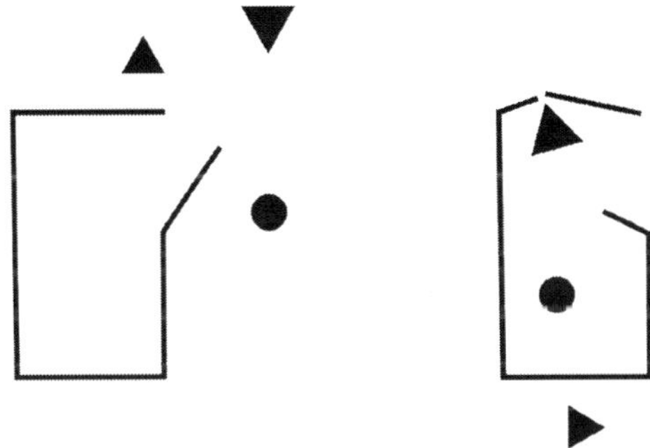

Figure 9.2: Heider and Simmel animation

Let's read a story:

Once upon a time, in a solitary house, lived a menacingly enormous triangle. One fateful day, as he peered outside, he observed a joyous couple passing by, a diminutive triangle and a petite circle. His fascination with the charming little circle was instant, captivating him with its beauty. Thus, he emerged from his dwelling and launched an assault on the petite triangle. Terrified, the tiny circle sought refuge within the house, while the little triangle gallantly defended himself. Alas, the colossal triangles might overwhelm the diminutive one, forcing him to retreat. With his competition dispatched, the large triangle returned home to claim his desired prize. The hapless little circle withdrew, while the giant triangle attempted to corner her. Meanwhile, the tiny triangle cautiously returned and gingerly opened the door of the house. Seizing the opportunity, the petite circle made a swift escape as the two of them cunningly locked the large aggressor inside. Overjoyed at their reunion, they merrily danced around each other. However, the formidable triangle managed to break free and pursue them around the house, but the little triangle and circle proved too swift, successfully evading capture. Left to his own devices, the colossal triangle succumbed to a fit of rage and demolished his abode in frustration.

You must look at this animation and build your own story to understand its perception in your own way. Good storytelling is a skill that can captivate and engage your audience, whether you are presenting your idea to a client, showcasing research insights and recommendations, giving a speech, or simply sharing a personal anecdote. Here are some tips for effective storytelling.

Tips on how to use storytelling effectively

Please follow the tips in the given table to make your storytelling effective:

- **Know your audience**: Empathy should be the core of your journey for storytelling. Knowing your audience's personality, demographics, and patterns about them, and then tailoring your story to their interests and expectations. You must consider their age, background, and interests when crafting your narrative.

Figure 9.3: Know your audience

- **Start with a strong hook**: As is rightly said, the first impression is the last impression. Build your first impression with an attention-grabbing start. Begin your story with an attention-grabbing opening that draws your audience in. This could be a question, a surprising fact, a compelling anecdote, or an exercise, and so on.

Figure 9.4: Start with a strong hook

- **Create relatable characters**: Everyone has their own learnings and experiences. People come with different cultures, so it is important to talk in the audience's language. Speak the language that audience will understand and relate with. Develop well-rounded and relatable characters that your audience can connect with emotionally. Readers or listeners should care about what happens to these characters.

Figure 9.5: *Create relatable characters*

- **Build a clear structure**: Define the structure well so that it is easier for the audience to consume the information you are going to present. Organize your story with a clear beginning, middle, and end. Introduce the setting, characters, and conflict early on, and then develop the plot to eventually resolve the conflict. Do not leave the story incomplete or leave any unconnected dots.

Figure 9.6: *Build a clear structure*

- **Show, do not tell**: As psychology says, pictures make a more impactful memory compared to text. So, use descriptive language and vivid imagery to allow your audience to visualize the story. Instead of telling them what is happening, show it through actions, dialogue, and sensory details. Let the audience consume the imagery and then convey the message by speaking. It will bring a bigger impact in your presentation.

Figure 9.7: Show, do not tell

- **Build suspense**: Keep your audience guessing by withholding information or hinting at future developments. This can create anticipation and intrigue. Due to this tension and suspense, the audience engages and asks questions as well. Make sure that you have answers to all the conflicting questions.

Figure 9.8: Build suspense

- **Provide resolution**: Make sure you are ready to answer all the possible questions. Conclude your story in a satisfying way that addresses the central conflict and provides closure for your characters. Do not leave the story incomplete; make sure to reach a conclusion or share your recommendation in case you are presenting some findings, learnings, or insights. Avoid leaving major questions unanswered.

Figure 9.9: Provide resolution

- **Practice, edit, and revise**: Writing is a process, so do not be afraid to revise and refine your story. Check for grammar and spelling errors, clarity, and coherence. The more you practice telling stories, the better you will become at it. Share your stories with friends or family to get feedback and hone your skills.

Figure 9.10: Practice, edit and revise

- **Be authentic**: Be authentic while presenting, be yourself, and share your own experiences, emotions, and perspectives. Authenticity can make your storytelling more relatable and powerful. Also, using real-life examples will make your story more practical and relatable. If you are presenting designs or research insights, make sure you talk about the complete process and effort behind them.

Figure 9.11: Be authentic

- **Listen to feedback**: Being an active listener is always the key to a great conversation, and when you are presenting, you should build that connection with the audience. So, pay attention to how your audience responds to your stories. Use their feedback to improve your storytelling techniques.

Figure 9.12: Listen to feedback

Conclusion

The storytelling effect is a power in the hands of the presenter to convey the message to the audience effectively, and to entertain, engage, and inspire. Storytelling helps the designers present the design effectively if the story has been built with facts, authenticity, and effort. This is a medium to convey the message, and it is one of the most important works of art after you develop your designs. It is always important to sell your ideas and solutions to stakeholders. We discussed how to be an effective storyteller in 10 steps. These steps will help you convince your stakeholders, as well as help you present your story/ideas with confidence. You will know the audience deeper and then you will be able to give a logical reason pertaining to your presentation. So, keep practicing those 10 steps of Storytelling and enhance your skills of presentation. With this, let us end this chapter and we will move to the next one.

In the next chapter, we are going to dive into another very important aspect of psychology in design, which is the *Halo effect*. This effect describes how people judge things (or people) based on their feelings towards one trait. See you in the next chapter!

Join our book's Discord space

Join the book's Discord Workspace for Latest updates, Offers, Tech happenings around the world, New Release and Sessions with the Authors:

https://discord.bpbonline.com

CHAPTER 10
Halo Effect

*"Why do favorable perceptions in one aspect positively
impact our opinions in other areas?"*

Introduction

The halo effect shapes your perceptions of others. It occurs when you instinctively form favorable opinions or assumptions about people due to a positive trait you observe in them. Despite having limited knowledge about these individuals, you subconsciously endow them with a halo of positivity, simply because they appear agreeable.

This effect is a type of stereotyping. It leads you to believe that all people who display a certain characteristic are alike, leading to assumptions that may not be accurate.

Structure

In this chapter, we are going to discuss the Halo effect, which is one of the greatest effects of psychology. We all do this unconsciously and do not even realize that we have assumed and judged someone, or something based on their beautiful or attractive appearance. We will discuss a few scenarios as well as how to use this psychological effect in UX design while designing a product.

The following topics will be covered:

- History
- Reverse Halo Effect
- Impact of Halo effect in UX Design

Objectives

The halo effect is a psychological phenomenon that helps us use first impressions and attractiveness to influence the decision or perception of the person who is observing you. Do you think we can use this psychological effect to make the experience of your product better or to increase the acquisition and retention of your product? Yes, we will learn the basics of Halo effect in this chapter and will explore how to use this effect to enhance your product design.

History

American psychologist *Edward L. Thorndike* pioneered research on the halo effect, a term he coined in 1920 following his studies with servicemen. In his experiments, commanding officers rated their subordinates on attributes like intelligence, physical appearance, leadership, and character without interacting with them. Thorndike observed a tendency to associate positive traits together; subordinates who were taller and more attractive were also perceived as more intelligent and competent soldiers. This led him to conclude that people often extrapolate a single prominent trait to form an overall positive impression of an individual's personality.

In 1946, *Solomon Asch*, a Polish-born psychologist, discovered that individuals' first impressions played a crucial role in forming their overall opinion of someone, a concept known as the primacy effect. This effect was demonstrated through an experiment where participants heard two lists of adjectives describing a person, with the order of the adjectives reversed in each list. The first list transitioned from positive to negative traits, while the second flipped this arrangement. The experiment revealed that the sequence of adjectives significantly influenced participants' perceptions. Adjectives heard early on had a greater impact than those heard later. Consequently, when the positive traits were listed first, participants formed a more favorable opinion of the person, whereas starting with negative traits led to a less favorable assessment. This study highlighted the disproportionate weight of initial information in shaping people's judgments of others. The halo effect is a type of cognitive bias suggesting that our positive perceptions of people, brands, or products in one aspect positively affect our opinions in other areas.

The term halo originates from a religious notion, symbolizing a ring of light around or above the head of a sacred figure, such as a saint, in recognition of their holiness. Many medieval and Renaissance paintings portray distinguished individuals adorned with this divine glow, encouraging viewers to perceive these figures positively.

These artistic depictions are akin to the psychological principle of the halo effect, as described by *Albert Ellis* in 2018 (*Albert Ellis* was a prominent psychologist known for his **cognitive-behavioral therapy (CBT)**). In this context, a prominent trait of an individual can lead observers to make sweeping judgments about them. Thus, a single positive attribute can create a favorable bias towards all aspects of a person, while a single *Negative Trait* can result in an overall negative perception.

Have you ever noticed the Halo effect in your own decision making? Imagine there is a new employee in the office who looks attractive by appearance. As of now, you have no idea about the educational or professional background she/he has,. However, have you ever assumed someone having a smart personality, merely based on their looks? You assume that his/her communication skills would be efficient, while them also having a positive and intelligent aura around the personality. However, you may at times meet a person and realize that your assumptions were not accurate.

This happens to all of us. We judge people, brands, and products by their first appearance and take it for face value. In India, there is a proverb in Hindi:

"जो दिखता है, वो बिकता है।"

(Whatever looks attractive, sells more)

But the reality is that we should *never judge a book by its cover*.

We notice a clear example of the halo effect here and it is not something that a person does intentionally. Our mind is designed in such a manner that we get biased by the halo effect. This is all done by our unconscious mind.

Since the halo effect is closely related to appearances, it plays a significant role in product branding and marketing. People often remain loyal to brands they have previously perceived as high-quality. For example, it is uncommon for someone to use different brands for their phone, computer, and watch. Once a brand earns our loyalty, it gains a *golden halo*, making it challenging for us to consider other options.

In the marketing world, have you ever noticed why brands take the help of celebrities, and public faces to convey the message to you? The promote an amazing product and show the celebrity endorsing it, use the same as well. This is all about Halo effect.

Companies exploit the halo effect by employing well-known public figures or conventionally attractive individuals to endorse their products, thereby reaching a broader audience and eliciting favorable brand evaluations. For instance, choosing a brand of running shoes might be influenced by advertisements featuring healthy, fit individuals or renowned athletes.

However, effective marketing does not always reflect the true quality of a product. In today's social media-driven world, we are bombarded with various marketing campaigns, each vying for our attention. Therefore, it is crucial to take a moment and make more considered decisions, rather than being quickly swayed by appealing images or endorsements. Consumers get attracted by celebrities and end up buying and using the product. That is the goal of the marketing team, to get the product to sell by using the halo effect.

Reverse Halo effect

The Reverse Halo effect, or Horns effect, is a cognitive bias where a person's negative overall impression negatively influences our perception of their specific traits or abilities. This effect is the antithesis of the halo effect, where positive impressions lead to positive perceptions.

In the reverse halo effect, an individual's negative traits or flaws can overshadow their positive qualities, resulting in skewed judgments and evaluations.

For example, the Horns effect might lead us to erroneously believe that someone who is physically overweight is lazy, despite no actual correlation between physical appearance and moral character.

Joseph Forgas' experiment involving 246 participants supports this notion. Participants were asked to recall either happy or sad memories before reading a philosophical essay attributed to either a young female or an old male author.

The study found that participants in a negative mood, having recalled sad events, gave lower ratings to the essay supposedly written by the young female, suggesting a negation or reversal of the halo effect.

Additionally, research indicates that both men and women who are deemed more attractive are often perceived as vainer and more egotistical (*Eagly, Ashmore, Makhijani & Longo,* 1991).

Moreover, as highlighted in the research by *Sigall* and *Ostrove*, individuals who exploit their attractiveness to commit crimes tend to receive harsher penalties compared to less attractive offenders (*Sigall & Ostrove,* 1975).

Impact of Halo Effect in UX

The halo effect can influence perceptions of organizations, places, products, and communication methods, as well as our views of others. If users favor one aspect of a website, application, or any digital product, they are more likely to have a positive overall opinion of it later. So, if the user likes the look and feel of the app or is somehow impressed by its first impression, it is very likely that they will assume that the service provided by this application will also be helpful while he might have no clue about the feedback on its services.

Referring to *Figure 10.1*, The user seems to be happy with the onboarding flow of a particular app but immediately that joy of experiencing a smooth onboarding generated the thoughts and assumptions that the other services (customer care, delivery, social media, and so on.) of the same app will be also great. That is how the halo effect works.

Figure 10.1: *Impressive First experience of an app builds a perception that the brand is great and trustworthy*

Imagine an e-commerce app you opened, and you were so impressed with the onboarding of the app and how the homepage appeared with information, you immediately liked the products. Hence, you have a good first impression, and now that perfect first impression of the app will lead your thoughts towards the other services of the app like delivery, customer care, and so on will be also of top notch. You will start trusting the app and will feel that the products here are all genuine. It is possible that you have no idea about the quality and services of the app. This is all about the impact of the halo effect. Have you ever experienced this?

On the other hand, if a user had a bad experience with a website or mobile app, they may anticipate future negative experiences and be hesitant to revisit them. This reluctance can persist even if the website/app improves, as users' prior negative impressions may linger. Refer to *Figure 10.2*, the user seems to have a bad experience of the app and that thought will lead the user to believe that the services provided by the app are also compromised.

***Figure 10.2:** Bad design of the app made the impression that the services will be bad too*

Have you ever gone through a website and exited immediately after looking at the first page or just after scrolling through the homepage? Or have you ever installed an app on your mobile device and uninstalled it immediately after spending some time on the mobile app? In these cases, you either did not have a good first impression or did not like something specific on the app homepage which tarnished its first impression. When the quality of an app's search results impact your perceptions of the app's overall quality and, consequently, of the associated brand and products, can also create reservations for you.

In a think-aloud study, a user might express frustration with poor search results, leading to a negative judgment of the site and the company, doubting its competence and customer care, and thus avoiding its products. While each step in this reasoning is somewhat logical, the conclusion does not necessarily follow from the initial observation. It is possible to receive a quality product from a site with inadequate search functionality. However, users often bypass a logical thought process due to the halo effect, forming overall judgments based on their initial impression of a single attribute.

This is the impact of the Horns effect, which is the reverse of the Halo effect. You judge the services and every aspect of the brand as bad and not worthy just because you had a bad first impression of the app or because you were not impressed by the search results of this e-commerce app.

Hence, after knowing all about the halo effect and the horns effect, what should a UX designer take care of while designing for the user or designing a product?

- **Design a smooth and easy onboarding process**: Your mobile app or website's onboarding is about the first impression of the app and making sure that you handhold your users for a short time so that the experience of getting acquainted with your brand and application, is top notch. If you have any glitches or miss making a good first impression, you miss an opportunity, and you may end up losing a user.

For example, I was going through the Zepto app (one of the grocery delivery apps in India) and was impressed by it is quick onboarding. Just asking for a mobile number, verification by OTP, and landing the user on the home screen, is a quick and efficient way to bridge the gap between users and the information/services. Refer to *Figure 10.3*, *Figure 10.4*, and *Figure 10.5* to observe how smooth and quick onboarding is:

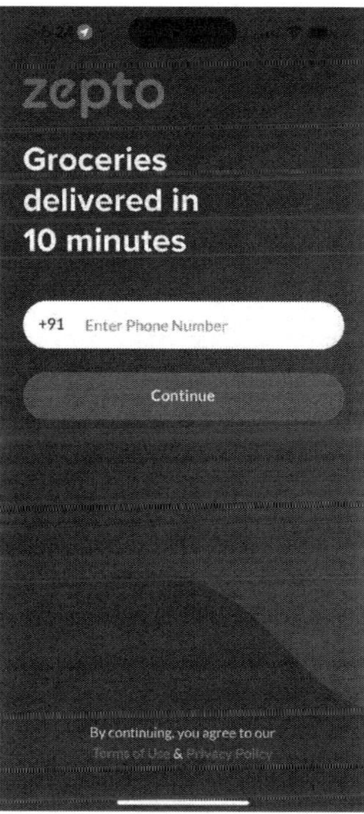

Figure 10.3: First screen of Zepto

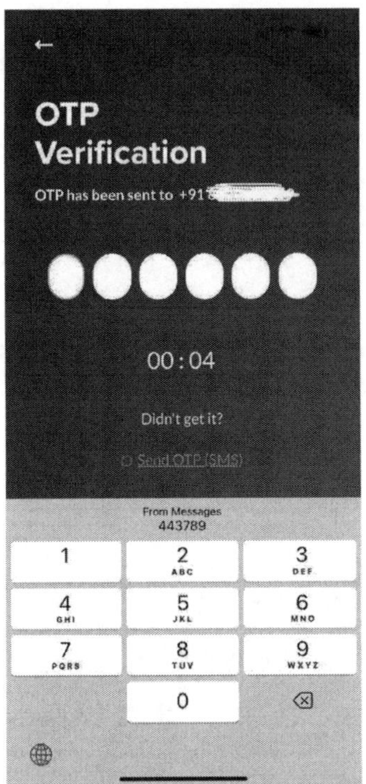

Figure 10.4: *OTP verification*

Figure 10.5: *Homepage of Zepto*

By having a smooth and less fractional onboarding process, brands can make a good first impression in the minds of the users. The halo effect gets implemented well; otherwise, your app will be impacted by the horns effect.

- **Focus on the visual of your app or website**: You may notice that a lot of apps and websites that do not compromise on their UI and visual design innovations. They are always refreshing their UI style, and their benchmarks for visuals are very high in comparison to the other apps available on the market.

The reason is very clear. They want to make an impact in their user's minds that they are interesting, rich in style, great in services, while taking care of their customers well. The moment your app or website looks attractive, you will definitely receive that applause and appreciation for your app and services. So as a UX/UI designer, make sure that the visuals of your digital platform are top-notch.

You may easily count a few Global and Indian apps that are famous for their design leadership; a few obvious names are: AirBnb, Myntra, Swiggy, Netflix, and so on. Refer to the *Figure 10.6, Figure 10.7, Figure 10.8*, and *Figure 10.9* to see their home screens:

o Airbnb has been famous for their clean UI and UI& UX innovations very often. The clean icons style, perfect alignment and few great interactions, does it all (refer to the following figure):

Figure 10.6: *Airbnb home screen*

o Netflix has been another example; they personalize their app/TV UI as per their user's taste and browsing behavior while experimenting their visuals (refer to the following figure):

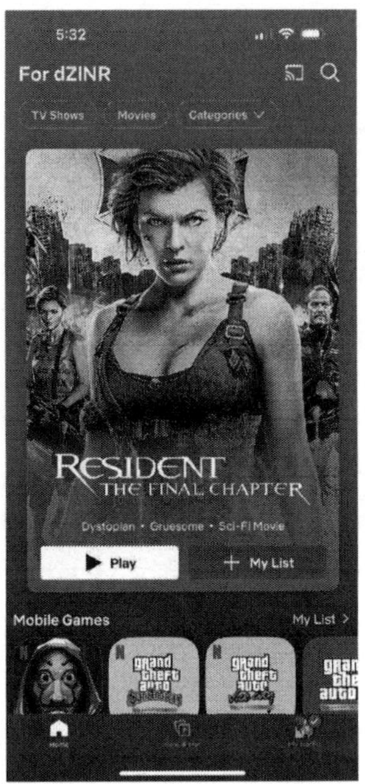

Figure 10.7: Netflix home screen

o   Myntra being a leading fashion e-commerce platform of India is also always innovating. Every few days you will notice a new feature or new pattern on their app regarding offerings, look or feel (refer to the following figure):

Figure 10.8: Myntra home screen

o   Swiggy is another great example, leading food delivery app in India. They are famous for their rich UI and interesting micro animations (refer to the following figure):

Figure 10.9: *Swiggy home screen*

With the help of attractive visuals, you always make a great first impression, means best use of the Halo effect.

Conclusion

Often, users evaluate digital products based on judgmental heuristics and cognitive biases. For instance, when you ask a friend about a site and they reply, *It's beautiful*, they are focusing on aesthetics rather than usability. This highlights why it is critical to consider and enhance all aspects of the halo effect during site or app development, flow design, KPI definition, and performance measurement. A drop-off at any stage could result in a negative first impression.

As an **user experience designer (UXD)**, it is your duty to use the Halo effect in the right manner and not get misguided by the Horns effect as this first impression of your digital product usually determines the journey of the user on your platform.

In the next chapter, we are going to learn about the goal gradient effect. This effect demonstrates how user's motivation goes up when the project/task is at the stage of completion. This is also a psychological effect that is being used in gamification, and it helps in building the experience in such a manner that users are excited to complete the task as soon as possible. Let us discuss more about this in the upcoming chapter.

Key findings

- The halo effect, also known as the halo error, is a cognitive bias where our overall impression of someone is influenced positively by our views of their other related characteristics.

- *Edward Thorndike*, an American psychologist, first documented the halo effect with empirical evidence in his 1920 article, *A Constant Error in Psychological Ratings*. This effect plays a role in shaping our judgments about others' intelligence and abilities and can be observed in various environments, from educational settings to legal proceedings.

- An instance of the halo effect is the attractiveness stereotype, which is the tendency to attribute positive qualities and traits to physically attractive individuals. Consequently, attractive people are often perceived to be more moral, mentally healthy, and intelligent. This judgmental error reflects an individual's biases, ideologies, and social perceptions.

- When planning sites, designing flows, setting **key performance indicators (KPIs)**, and measuring your site's performance, it is crucial to consider the halo effect. This is because the drop-offs at any stage of the user experience could signal a negative initial impression caused by design, content, or site performance issues.

- Conversely, the reverse halo effect occurs when positive impressions of a person lead to adverse outcomes.

- Related to the halo effect is the horn effect, a cognitive bias where a single negative trait disproportionately influences our overall opinion of someone.

Join our book's Discord space

Join the book's Discord Workspace for Latest updates, Offers, Tech happenings around the world, New Release and Sessions with the Authors:

https://discord.bpbonline.com

Chapter **11**

Goal Gradient Effect

"As one gets closer to a goal, the inclination to reach it intensifies."

Introduction

The Goal Gradient Effect is a psychological phenomenon that suggests individuals are increasingly motivated to reach a goal as they get closer to it. This concept, rooted in behavioral psychology, implies that the closer one perceives themselves to achieving a goal, the more effort and enthusiasm they tend to exhibit.

For example, in the context of consumer behavior, customers participating in a loyalty program might accelerate their purchases as they approach the threshold for a reward. Similarly, a runner might increase their speed as they get near the finish line in a race.

Structure

In this chapter, we will deep dive and understand the Goal Gradient effect. How does this effect motivate the user when he/she is near the completion of the task or near the finishing line. There is extra layer of intrinsic motivation that is produced during this moment to finish the task. We will also discover how this effect is used in the world of digital platform to motivate the users to complete a task as soon as possible. This chapter covers the below topics:

- History
- Goal gradient effect in UX
- Practical examples of Goal gradient effect

Objectives

The Goal gradient effect is a psychological effect that proves that an individual gets motivated to complete the task once it is near completion. In this chapter we will discuss how this effect can help the designers motivate their users to use their product and complete a specific task. After learning this effect, you will be able to apply the learnings of this effect and help your product to get better acquisition and retention.

History of the goal gradient effect

The goal-gradient theory, first introduced by behaviorist *Clark Hull* in 1932, suggests that the closer one is to a goal, the stronger is the drive to achieve it. *Hull* demonstrated this in 1934 through an experiment where rats ran faster in a straight alley as they neared food. While this hypothesis has been widely explored in animal behavior (refer to works by Anderson 1933, Brown 1948, and a review by *Heilizer* 1977), (**https://psycnet.apa.org/record/1934-04965-001**) its relevance to human behavior and decision-making remains less examined. Moreover, this concept holds significant; theoretical and practical value for understanding consumer behavior over time, particularly in **reward programs (RPs)** and various motivational systems, as discussed in studies by *Deighton* 2000, *Hsee* 2003, *Kivetz* 2003, Lal and Bell 2003 (various research in this field has already been done. One of the links you can use to learn more is **https://journals.sagepub.com/doi/10.1509/jmkr.43.1.39**)

Figure 11.1: An athlete about to complete the race

Imagine an athlete participating in an Olympic 1600-meter sprint. During the initial two laps, he maintains a strong, steady pace, aiming to stay at the forefront or at least in the middle of the group. His strategy is not to lag too far behind while also saving energy for the entire race.

By the 800-meter mark, he starts to feel weary, and his speed decreases. At 1000 meters, there is a noticeable reduction in his energy output. After reaching 1200 meters, doubts about his training adequacy creep in.

Observe him as he enters the final 100 meters—the intense race to the finish line. He has already been sprinting at a pace extraordinary for most people for 1500 meters. Yet, as he finds himself shoulder to shoulder with his rivals, the finish line within grasp, something changes.

He accelerates. The slump in energy vanishes. The end goal is imminent, requiring just one final surge of effort and so he gives it his all.

This phenomenon is known as the Goal Gradient Effect, or more accurately, the Goal Gradient Hypothesis. It is not just a psychological effect; it has tangible, measurable impacts on biological beings.

As individuals approach their objective, they begin to envision the sensation of accomplishment. Consider the athlete rounding the final bend and catching sight of the finish line. This vision fuels their anticipation, propelling them to sprint with all their might, knowing the reward is imminent upon completion.

This sense of anticipation activates a surge of dopamine, a neurotransmitter associated with enjoyment and drive. The release of dopamine occurs during enjoyable experiences, such as savoring tasty food or getting a social media alert. This pleasurable sensation encourages individuals to exert greater effort when the end goal is within their grasp.

> *"The anticipation mechanism triggers a rush of dopamine, a brain chemical linked to pleasure and motivation. The feeling of pleasure motivates the user to apply extra effort and achieve the goal"*
>
> — *Noah Kagan*

This brings us to a very important point that the goal gradient effect is connected with a reward. The participant puts extra effort into completing the task because he / she can imagine the reward once they complete.

If you remember the previous *Chapter 8, Ziagarnik Effect*, we discussed that incomplete tasks remain in your memory and keep reminding you sub-consciously that you need to complete them. Goal gradient effect is slightly inspired from the Ziagarnik Effect as well. Since your mind keeps reminding you of the task left and you can anticipate the reward at the end of the task. Users end up getting motivated.

Individuals often find it easier to recall pending tasks rather than those they have accomplished. Incomplete duties tend to linger more prominently in their thoughts, overshadowing completed ones, as their focus shifts to future actions required to achieve their objectives.

This mental inclination intensifies as they draw nearer to their goal, heightening their consciousness of remaining tasks. This heightened awareness motivates them to exert additional effort to complete these tasks and attain their desired objective.

> *"Rats run faster as they approach a food reward."*

> — *Hull, 1934*

Practical examples of Goal gradient effect

The goal gradient effect is such an impactful effect to apply in your designs to motivate the users to complete the task. There is power in progress and when an individual knows the progress of the effort, he/she is putting in, it boosts motivation. There could be multiple ways to show the individual's progress. Refer to *Figure 11.2*, where you will see the progress of a user showcased by a progress bar. The progress of multiple tasks is shown in multiple progress bars:

Figure 11.2: Showcasing the progress to the users

When a user is aware of the progress of all the tasks, he/she is doing, and if those are near completion, that itself is motivational. The preceding figure is just a simple progress report.

Another progress report could be a report with milestone information. Referring to *Figure 11.3*, you will notice that it shows the progress of one goal only, but that one goal has multiple milestones in its journey. These small milestones give the users the effect of the goal gradient. If there was only one bigger goal, it would feel like an individual would need to put in a lot of effort to complete such a huge task, and might lose motivation multiple times in the process, which may cause this task to remain incomplete.

However, milestones introduce the wonder of this process. A milestone breaks a bigger goal into multiple smaller chunks. Now the user will target to achieve those smaller goals one by one, and it will drive the motivation to finish one goal and target for the next one. Refer to *Figure 11.3* where the goal is divided into 4 milestones.

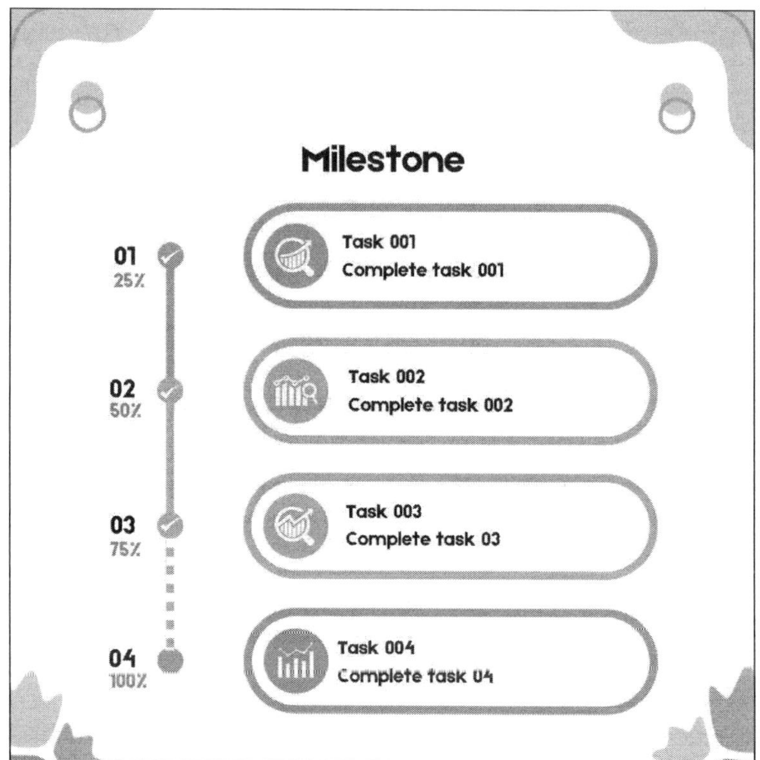

Figure 11.3: *Showcasing the progress of a goal with multiple smaller milestone*

Since the above goal is divided into 4 milestones of 25% each, with the help of the goal gradient effect, it is highly likely that users will complete all said tasks. Hence, what we are learning here is that breaking bigger goals into multiple milestones boosts motivation. And adding reward with every milestone boosts it further.

Bonus events can help increase customer goal-gradient behavior toward reaching a reward.

Myntra (a well-known fashion e-commerce site in India) uses the goal gradient effect so well. For their Insider program, which is their membership plan, you upgrade as per your purchase, and every tier gives you better advantages as per the level.

Refer to *Figure 11.4*, which is the Myntra Insider Dashboard. They use the progress bar to inform the users about their Tier and milestone level when they achieve or are about to reach them. This helps the users be informed about the progress as well as motivates them to do some more purchases and achieve next-tier tiers like Elite or Icon.

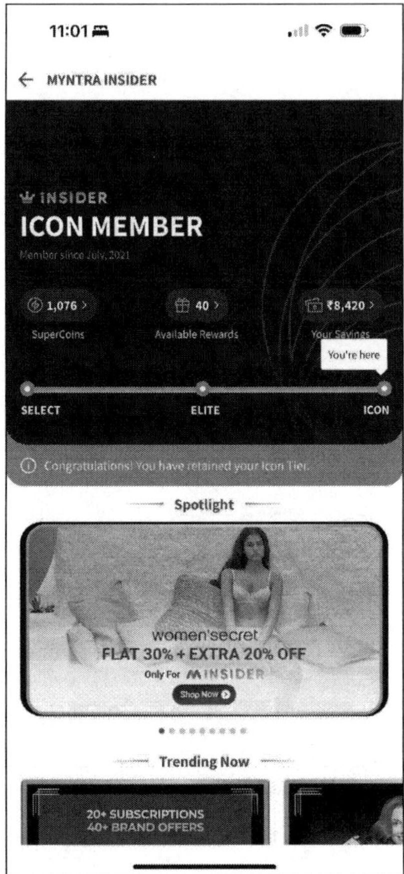

Figure 11.4: Myntra Insider Progress bar

Not only does Myntra's dashboard remind the users about their progress after every purchase (for example, if you spend INR 1,000 more, you will be upgraded to Insider Elite), it showcases the benefits of being an Elite Member. This is a perfect example of motivating users with the goal-gradient effect.

Let us look at a few real-life examples of how few digital platforms use the progress bar to drive engagement and user retention.

Let us check out another example from another digital platform. MakeMyTrip, which is another very famous app. It is an aggregator of travel and holiday package booking. They also have their membership plan called **MMT BLACK**. They have 3 tier of the users that are preferred, elite and exclusive. Exclusive being the topmost in the hierarchy. Refer to *Figure 11.5* to check the Dashboard of MakeMyTrip. It indicates the progress through a progress bar. It also conveys information about how much effort is needed to hit the next level of membership and what benefits you get when you achieve a particular hierarchy.

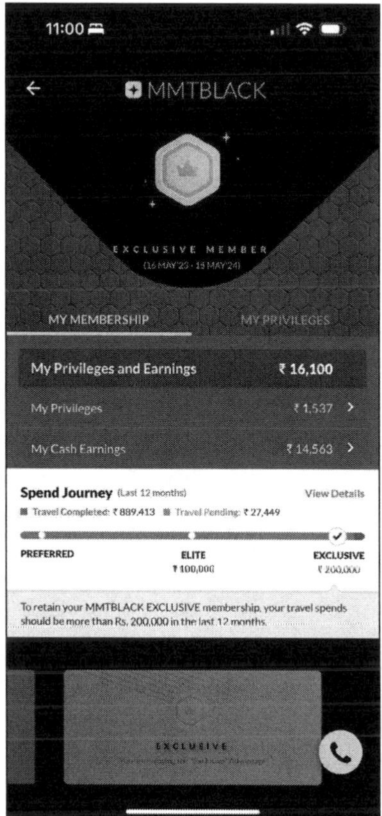

Figure 11.5: *MakeMyTrip MMTBLACK membership plan Dashboard*

This is again a great example of Goal gradient effect where MakeMyTrip motivates their users to do more transactions on their app, spend more time, book more flights, hotels and holidays. And as a result, Users gain some extra points. Those points help users to upgrade their MMT Black Membership.

When users reach a certain level of membership, they can enjoy additional benefits like Free Airport pick and drop, Early check-in in hotels and some more extra facilities as reward.

The rewards are also planned in such a manner that they will influence the users to spend more and upgrade their membership.

In this example you see the usage of milestone to inform the users about the progress as well as the reward to motivate the users to spend more and achieve the next goal.

Another example is from the gaming world. An example from the game Royal Match Usually this is very common in most new games where one is targeting a particular goal and that end goal is divided into multiple milestones. Here, players are motivated enough to achieve every milestone of the goal. When you refer to *Figure 11.6,* it has a screenshot of the Royal Match game in which you can see a progress bar at the top that denotes the achievements, which are collectibles. You will also notice there are a few collectibles below, which are Royal, Backyard, Library, and Summer. You will notice that these are divided into chunks, or, as you may call them, streaks. You will complete every collectible in nine parts after you complete a task. There comes a time when you had been achieving streaks for multiple collectibles as rewards, and that has kept you motivated to play more and keep achieving more streaks.

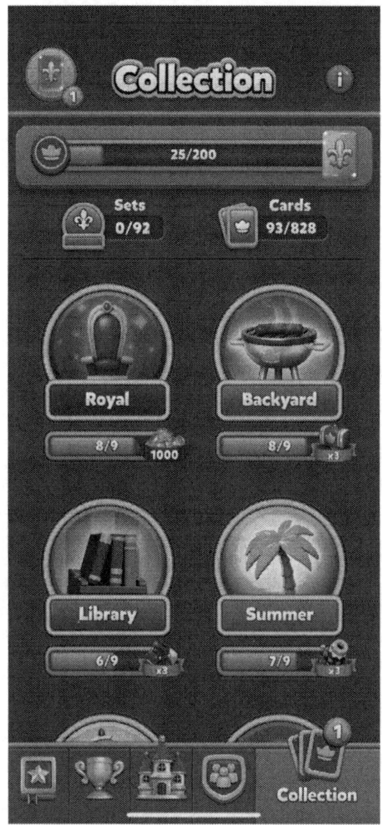

Figure 11.6: Royal match progression and collection in streaks

The example where the players collect these collectibles (Royal, Backyard, Library, Summer) – Refer to *Figure 11.6*, are a good example of the goal gradient effect. You are being rewarded for collecting different rewards at the same time and you keep getting rewarded once one of the streaks/reward is completed.

If you observe the reward and task completion mechanisms in most games, you will realize that the Gradient effect is the most used psychological phenomena to motivate the users.

Gamification is something that you will learn in subsequent chapters, but be assured that the fundamentals of gamification and the goal gradient effect have been very commonly used on most digital platforms these days to drive more engagement. I am going to discuss a few specific Gamification topics in the upcoming chapters, where we will discuss deeply about scarcity, positive and negative reinforcement, reciprocation, and social shared commitment.

Conclusion

To effectively motivate people, we must concentrate on highlighting how close they are to receiving a reward. Positively reinforce desired behaviors and vary the timing and predictability of these rewards.

Make sure that progress indicators are conspicuous and align with the ultimate goal in registration and checkout processes. The perception of progress is a powerful motivator. Start by indicating progress from the very first step of your form or checkout.

Utilizing the goal-gradient effect in free trial periods can be advantageous. Regular updates to users about the remaining time before the trial expires can encourage them to upgrade. This strategy emphasizes the urgency and the limited time left before they lose access to the service.

I hope you learned and will use this effect while designing your next product and will try to motivate your users with the goal gradient effect.

In the next chapter, we are going to discuss the impact of a picture on their memory and how it helps to recall the stuff. Yes, this effect is called the **Picture Superiority Effect**, and this is another important psychological effect that you may use very often in your design to make sure that you get the user's attention and make sure that users will memorize your product and experience.

See you in the next chapter!

Join our book's Discord space

Join the book's Discord Workspace for Latest updates, Offers, Tech happenings around the world, New Release and Sessions with the Authors:

https://discord.bpbonline.com

CHAPTER 12

Picture Superiority Effect

"People remember pictures better than words."

Introduction

The **Picture Superiority Effect (PSE)** describes the tendency of individuals to recall images more effectively than the associated words. This means that, in terms of memory recall and recognition, images are more impactful than words.

The principle of the picture superiority effect is versatile and can be applied in various scenarios. For instance, to remember to buy items like sour cream and shredded cheese, visualizing a taco topped with these ingredients might be more effective than trying to recall a written list.

This example illustrates just one everyday application of the picture superiority effect. Additionally, the concept encompasses the enhanced recall of information when it is presented visually rather than textually. According to *Brain Rules* (a book written by *John Medina* that explains how our brains work and applies this knowledge), people typically remember just 10% of what they read or hear after three days. But when an image accompanies the information, their recall rate jumps to 65 percent.

This insight is particularly valuable for entrepreneurs, business owners, bloggers, and marketers. They can leverage this concept in branding and marketing, as well as in explaining complex subjects using visuals like charts and infographics.

Structure

The picture superiority effect is another important psychological effect and a concept of cognitive psychology that demonstrates how pictures impact your memory more than textual or other stuff. In this chapter, we will understand this effect deeply and also discuss the digital examples where it is being applied, and we all have been experiencing that, knowingly or unknowingly. We will also discuss the impactful implementation of this effect and tips for using it in your Designs. This chapter will cover the following topics, as mentioned:

* History of PSE
* Know what makes images memorable

Objectives

The picture superiority effect is a gift for all designers, which they must use to make their work impactful. After reading this chapter, you will be able to use this effect impactfully in your design. You will understand the value of text (copy) and the value of images/pictures in your design. How it grabs attention, and after grabbing attention, it stays for a long time in the user's memory. Hence, if you want your users to remember your design and the message, you must use the picture superiority effect very carefully.

In this chapter, you will understand:

* History of PSE
* What makes images memorable

History of PSE

The **Picture Superiority Effect (PSE)**, a concept in cognitive psychology and memory studies, has a fascinating history rooted in research on human memory and information processing. While the term itself might not have been used historically, the underlying concept has been explored for decades.

* **Early research and foundations:** The roots of PSE can be traced back to early research in the 20th century on imagery and memory. Pioneering psychologists like *Allan Paivio* in the 1960s and 1970s contributed significantly with his Dual Coding Theory. This theory proposes that both verbal and non-verbal processing are essential for cognition and that imagery (or non-verbal processing) plays a key role in memory retention.

* **Paivio's Dual Coding Theory:** *Allan Paivio's* work was crucial in laying the groundwork for understanding how people process and remember information. He argued that information could be encoded into memory in two ways: either as verbal descriptions or as visual images. His experiments showed that people tend to recall information better if it is presented both visually and verbally, compared to just one of the modalities.

- **Further experiments and expansion:** Throughout the 1970s and 1980s, numerous experiments were conducted that supported and expanded upon *Paivio's* theory. These experiments consistently showed that participants could remember pictures more easily and accurately than words.

- **Neuroscientific advances:** With the advent of neuroimaging techniques in the late 20th and early 21st centuries, researchers were able to explore the neural correlates of the PSE. They discovered that different areas of the brain are activated during processing of visual and verbal materials, supporting the idea of dual coding.

- **Modern applications:** In recent years, the Picture Superiority Effect has found applications in various fields, including marketing, education, and user interface design. It is used to enhance memory retention and user engagement, leveraging the fact that visuals are more likely to be remembered than text alone.

Let us ask ourselves a few questions and understand a pattern. In the following table, check type I and II, and think of your preference:

Type - I	Type - II
A page with only text	**A page with minimal text and lot of images**

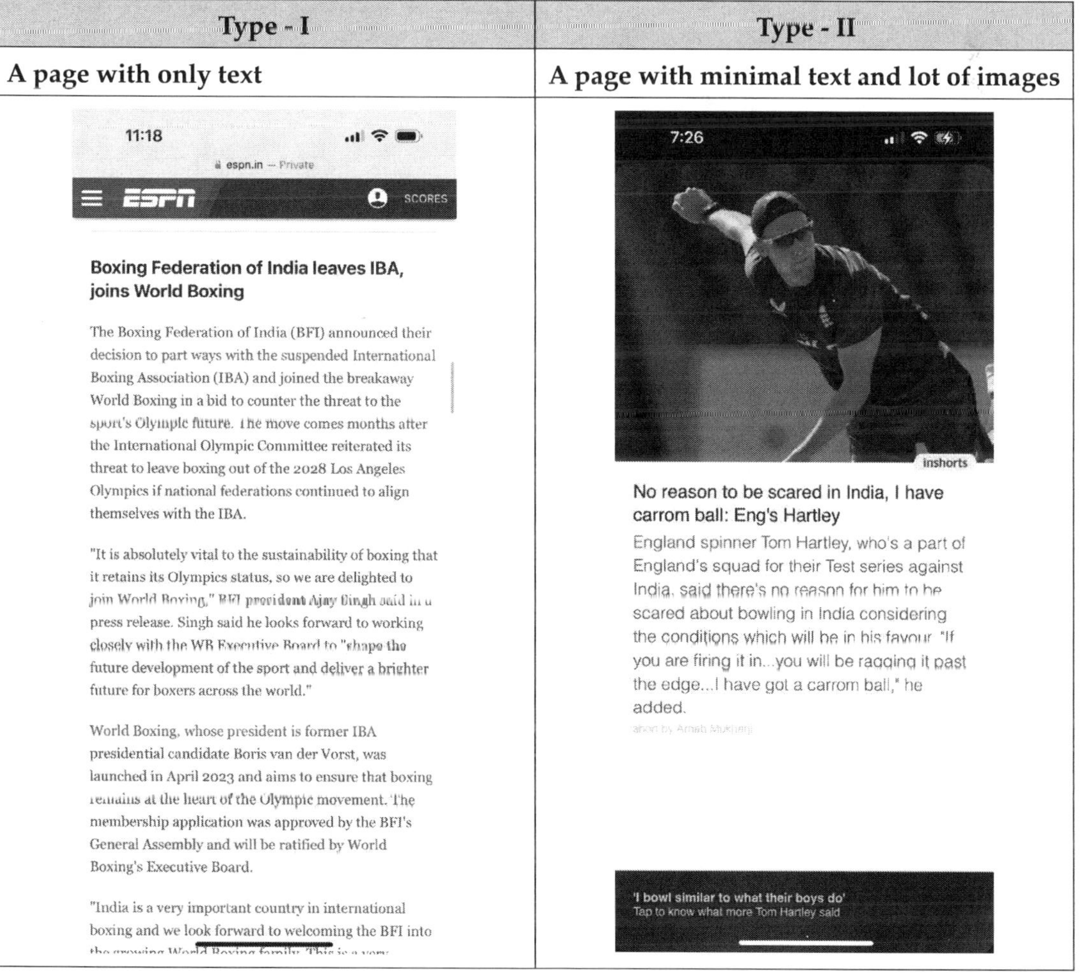

Type - I	Type - II
A news screen with three paragraphs of text and a headline.	A news screen with self-explanatory image and a supporting one liner copy.

Table 12.1: Instances of PSE

If you analyze the table now, Type II is more relatable and has better readability.

Let us now understand why that is. This is the **Picture Superiority Effect**. It is always preferred to be more comfortable consuming pictures than text/copy. The biggest reason for this is that pictures stay longer in our memory.

The Picture Superiority Effect continues to be a topic of research and exploration, particularly as it highly relates to how modern technologies and digital media can be used to enhance learning and memory. Its history reflects the evolving understanding of how we process, store, and retrieve information.

Let us understand the basics of memory. There are three types of memories.

- **Sensory memory:** When a human looks at something, that thing stays in human memory for just a fraction of a second. Eyes and mind notice it, and it's saved in sensory memory.

- **Short-term memory**: It stays in our mind for 15 to 30 seconds, depending on the frequency of repetitive rehearsal of the information.

- **Long-term memory:** This can be retained indefinitely. Strength and retention depend on several factors, such as the emotional significance of the memory, rehearsal, frequency of recall, and so on.

The moment we look at some information as text or image, it goes to our sensory memory, and if it is noticeable or impactful, it is transferred to short term or long-term memory, depending upon how much we have memorized and practiced it. A few impactful things stay in one's memory longer, like a picture. Pictures usually have more value of recall and the probability of staying that in our memory is higher because of picture's properties. Pictures easily go to short term and long-term memory compared to text only.

However, all kinds of pictures/images are not impactful and do not go into short term and long-term memory.

Know what makes images memorable

Not all images have the same impact on memory. As described by MIT, the memorability of an image can vary depending on the user's context and individual differences. Generally, human faces and indoor settings are more memorable than outdoor landscapes.

Moreover, images that combine an object with a scene are more likely to be remembered. This means that while the image should highlight a specific object, it should not be so zoomed in that the surrounding environment is lost.

For instance, when selecting a photo or headshot for social media use, opt for one that showcases both your face and some background elements, as discussed further.

Refer to *Figure 12.3*. It is a picture with no background, or a flat background, which is gray. It looks good as a professional photograph, but it is highly likely that this image will not have an impact on the user's memory. Since there is no memorable background, users tend not to focus a lot on this image, and it will be less impactful:

Figure 12.3: *An AI generated picture with no background*

Now you refer to *Figure 12.4*. This picture has a background of an office with a window showcasing outside greenery and garden. This background helps you build a story around it, while it is transferred from your sensory memory to short-term and long-term memory. It stays longer in your memory because it has a background. The office and garden in the background is enough for you to remember this image in the future.

Figure 12.4: *A picture with the background of Greenery, window and more noticeable stuff*

"The whole point of taking pictures is so that you don't have to
explain things with words."

— *Elliott Erwitt*

So, let us discuss the do's and don'ts with regards to the usage of pictures are for better recall in the user's mind. There are a few kinds of images that are good for user recall. Objects that are most memorable to people typically encompass the following:

- Individuals
- Interior scenes
- Elements in the foreground
- Objects of a human scale

Conversely, objects that are less likely to be remembered including the following:

- External views
- Broad, wide-angle landscapes
- Background elements
- Natural settings

There are also a few rules for using images. If you are using a human picture, for example, if you are designing a banner for your landing page or mobile screen and your banner contains a human image, some text, and a button **Call to Action (CTA)**. The composition or arrangement of the elements (Text, image, button) of the banner should be in such a manner that it helps you achieve your goal of designing the banner.

Let us observe *Figure 12.5*. It is a banner for a social media campaign where the model is looking towards the user/customer, simultaneously grabbing the attention of the user. Many designers and brands use images like these to grab the attention of their customers. But there is a psychological effect that when a model/person is looking at the user, the user tends to miss the text in the banner. Hence, it is possible that users will notice the lady in the banner, but there is a high probability that users will miss the copy *Beauty Center* in the banner.

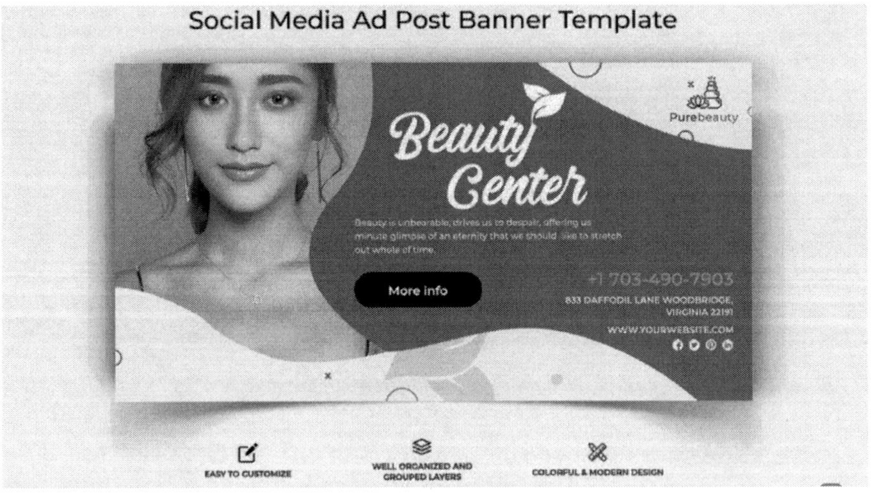

Figure 12.5: A Banner where the model is looking in front (in your eyes)

Now, when you notice *Figure 12.6*, you will observe that the model in the picture is not looking at you (the user), but the user is looking towards the text written on the banner.

Figure 12.6: *A banner, where the model is looking towards the copy/text*

This is another psychological effect that occurs when the model in the design or banner is looking at the text written there. It is highly likely that the user's attention goes to the text written on the banner first.

It is another way of highlighting the information in the banner. Hence, choose the picture as per your goal.

Conclusion

The picture superiority effect is a psychological phenomenon that refers to the impact that a picture creates on a user's mind compared to text. Pictures are more likely to be remembered, and they are easier to recall. That is why we say that designers must use pictures in their designs if they are looking for better recall for their designs.

Hence, few of the lessons for the designers are:

- Use self-explanatory pictures in your designs for better recall by the users.

- All images are not impactful and there are only a few types that are memorable.
- Pictures with some background are more memorable compared to flat or no background images.
- Pictures of individuals and interior scenes are more memorable.
- Pictures of a landscape, natural things, and so on, are less memorable.

I hope you learned and will use this effect while designing your next product and will try to get the attention of your users with the picture superiority effect.

In the next chapter, we are going to discuss the Von Restorff Effect, which conveys that the more something stands out, the higher is the probability of it being seen.

See you in the next chapter!

Join our book's Discord space

Join the book's Discord Workspace for Latest updates, Offers, Tech happenings around the world, New Release and Sessions with the Authors:

https://discord.bpbonline.com

CHAPTER 13

Von Restorff Effect

"The more it stands out, the higher the probability of being seen."

Introduction

The Von Restorff effect, commonly referred to as the isolation effect, suggests that in a group of similar items, the one that stands out or is different is the most likely to be remembered.

The Von Restorff Effect has been influential in various fields such as marketing, user interface design, and education. It is used to explain why unique or unusual advertisements are more likely to be remembered than common ones. Moreover, it is also applied in educational strategies to highlight key information. Additionally, in user interface design, it helps to explain why buttons or links that stand out are more likely to be noticed and clicked by users.

Structure

In this chapter, we are going to learn deeply about the Von Restorff Effect. We will understand how it is used on any digital platform and, as designers, how we can use this effect to get the attention of the users, with a few real-life examples.

The chapter discusses the following topics:

- History
- Von Restorff effects everyone
- Use of Von Restorff effect by UX Designers

Objectives

The Von Restorff effect is an important asset for designers to get the attention of their users. The designers must know how and when to use this effect to draw attention to a specific element of the design. After reading this chapter, you will be able to identify the Von Restorff effect on digital platforms and will be able to use it in your designs.

History

The Von Restorff Effect, also known as the isolation effect, was first identified by German psychiatrist and pediatrician *Hedwig von Restorff* in 1933. This psychological phenomenon is based on her research, which demonstrated that when multiple similar objects are presented, the one that differs from the rest is more likely to be remembered.

Von Restorff conducted several experiments to understand how memory works. In one of her most notable experiments, she presented participants with a list of categorically similar items with one distinctive, isolated item on the list. She found that the item that differed from the rest—whether in color, size, or shape—was more frequently recalled than the others. This effect occurs because the distinctiveness of the isolated item makes it stand out and, therefore, more memorable.

This effect is closely related to and sometimes overlaps with other cognitive biases and effects, such as the salience effect and the novelty effect, which also describe how distinctive or novel stimuli can capture our attention more effectively than familiar or common ones.

Figure 13.1: A pile of products and Horlicks seems big and highlighted

Just have a look at the above *Figure 13.1* and notice a pile of Grocery items in the picture, you will notice some packaged food items, fruits like bananas, grapes, and so on. But, what was the first thing in you noticed? It is Horlicks. It is so because the box is extremely highlighted as compared to other grocery items in the picture.

This is how the Von Restorff effect works, something that is highlighted, big and bold, gets more attention, and the probability of being seen is way higher as compared to others.

The Von Restorff effect can enhance memory retention of specific information within a group of data when applied effectively.

So now, it is easier for you to remember that you saw a picture of Horlicks surrounded by a group of packaged groceries and a few fruits. Now since you see above picture where Horlicks is highlighted, now whenever you describe this picture to someone, You will also emphasize Horlicks while describing compared to other grocery items in the picture. This effect helps you memorize the most important information, and if it is used effectively, you will be able to get some space for your product's retention in the user's mind.

Let us think of another scenario, you might be passing through a busy market. Imagine you crossed a market sometime back, which is a bit crowded and full of a lot of Billboards, and shops. Have a look at *Figure 13.2*. Do you think you will be able to remember a few shop names or a few billboard names when you see something like this??

Naturally, it is difficult to remember something in this scenario. Here, every billboard is trying to fight with each other to get the attention of the shoppers.

Figure 13.2: *A busy market with lot of billboards in the market*

Now, if you have a look at *Figure 13.3*, it is a similar busy market with a billboard full of things that are difficult to notice, but there is one difference. You can easily identify a highlighted Billboard out of so many. There are multiple reasons, one of which is that it is big and bold. Moreover, there is extra light on it. So, just making it bigger and bolder is not the way to highlight it and grab attention. There are multiple aspects that can be used to make things stand out. For example, the lights here. There could have been music and a few other elements as well.

Figure 13.3: A busy market with lot of billboards in the market but one highlighted

The Von Restorff effect can be used everywhere, not just on billboards. Few more elements produce the Von Restorff effect, like:

- Color
- Size
- Shape
- Motion
- Orientation

Von Restorff affects everyone

Let us look at a few examples in our real life where we experience this effect:

- **Highlighting texts in a book/notebook:** Frequently, people use highlighters on key sections of a book or document. The bright colors draw your eye to these parts, making them stand out and aiding in their recall compared to the rest of the text.

- **Memorable billboards:** On a highway peppered with billboards, the ones you remember are often those with an unusual design, striking color, or an engaging phrase. Their unique features help them stick in your memory. We have already discussed this phenomenon.

- **Distinctive fashion choice:** Have you spotted someone in a crowd wearing a vividly colored accessory, like a hat or shoes, amidst mostly neutral tones? This fashion choice leverages the Von Restorff Effect, ensuring they are remembered.

- **App notification badges:** Many apps use red badges to signal new messages or updates. These badges contrast with regular app icons, drawing your attention and making you more likely to check those apps.

- **Eye-catching sales promotions:** Retailers often employ bright, contrasting colors or flashing signs for short-term deals. These standout features help ensure that these offers catch your eye among a multitude of other items.

- **Personalized ringtones:** Setting a unique ringtone for certain contacts can help you instantly recognize the caller. This distinct sound makes it easier to recall who called, even long after the call.

Comprehending and identifying the Von Restorff Effect across different situations enables you to acknowledge its impact on your memory and utilize it efficiently in a range of professional and personal settings.

Use of Von Restorff effects by UX Designers

You do not need to be an expert in **user experience (UX)** design or marketing to leverage the Von Restorff effect in your communication. If you have an important message to share, it is worth considering how this effect can enhance your materials. Here are some practical suggestions for applying this effect effectively:

- Think about the devices your audience will use to view your content. For instance, devices like some Kindles display content in black and white, making color changes ineffective. Instead, you can vary other elements to make your content pop.

- Be judicious in what you choose to emphasize. If too much content is highlighted, nothing truly stands out.

- If everything is highlighted, the user will struggle to focus on something, so you must consider a good information architecture. Highlight the elements as per their hierarchy and priority.

- You may choose to highlight some stuff as per business requirements or to help the users narrow down their search process and make the decision quickly. You may see a similar example in *Figure 13.4*, A particular plan is highlighted, and I will talk about it in subsequent paragraphs.

- Experiment with different aspects of the effect through A/B testing. Observe whether your audience responds better to variations in color, size, style, or motion to distinguish information.

For instance, let us look at the live digital platform example. Have a look at the hosting plans offered by *Hostinger*. Refer to *Figure 13.4* (**Hostinger.com** plans to host a website). This is a comparison of all three plans. The Von Restorff effect is used to motivate the user's decision by making them believe that the central plan is the best. Although, it may not be the cheapest plan and does not have all the features. However, users figured out that this may be the plan that sells more, so the service providers are highlighting it, and users end up choosing that option.

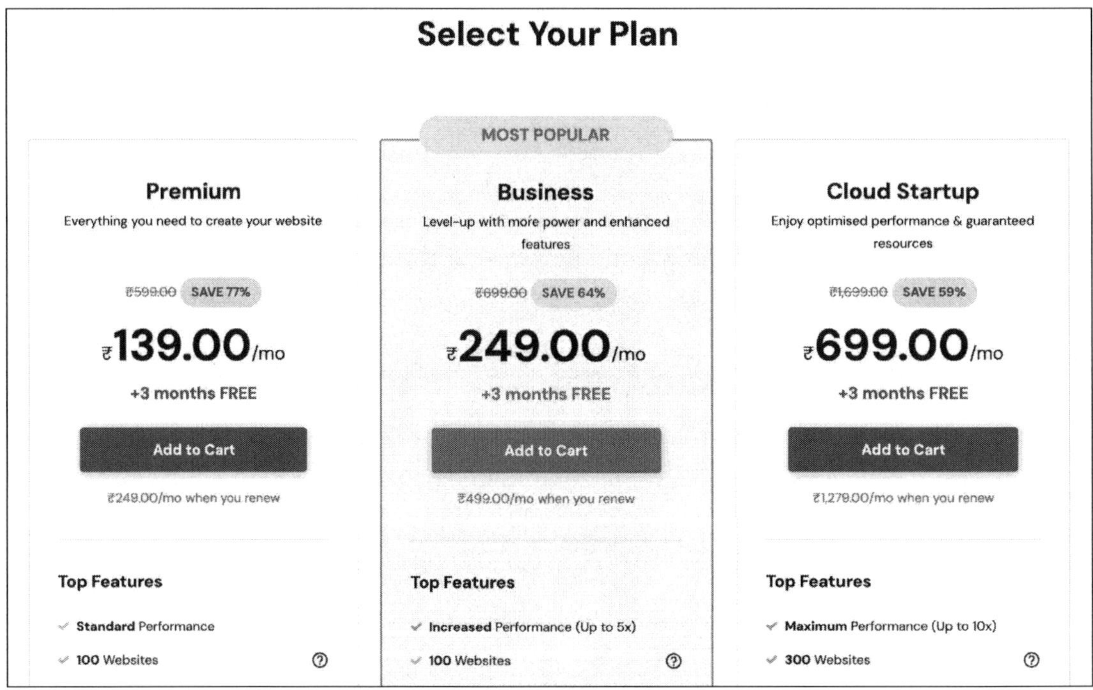

Figure 13.4: Website hosting plans of Hostinger

Conclusion

All of us experience the Von Restorff effect in our day to day life knowingly or unknowingly. From highlighting to wearing a unique outfit to having a unique ringtone in our mobile phones is all about the von Restorff effect.

It is also a unique proposition to be used in designs. It could be Graphic Design while designing a poster or a website or app or any kind of digital design too. As a designer, you always have to focus on your information hierarchy and must highlight the elements as per their priority so that it helps the users to consume the information.

While highlighting, you must consider not overdoing things, like not highlighting most of the stuff or every element. Consider people who could be visually impaired or motion-sensitive.

With this, we are done with all the psychological effects that we all experience and get used to. In the upcoming few chapters, we are going to understand an important part of design and see a lot of myths around that as well. We are going to discuss Gamification, and a few elements of this concept in detail with some examples. It helps in motivating and engaging our users.

Points to remember

- Ensure that crucial information or primary actions are visually prominent.
- Exercise caution in emphasizing visual elements to prevent them from overshadowing each other and to avoid the misperception of significant items as advertisements.
- Avoid depending solely on color to denote contrast, considering individuals with color vision deficiencies or low vision.
- Use multiple elements like color, size, shape, motion, and orientation to highlight your important information.
- Be mindful of users with motion sensitivity when employing movement to convey contrast.

Join our book's Discord space

Join the book's Discord Workspace for Latest updates, Offers, Tech happenings around the world, New Release and Sessions with the Authors:

https://discord.bpbonline.com

Section III
Gamification

Gamification refers to the application of game-design elements and principles in non-game contexts to enhance user engagement, motivation, and overall experience. In design, gamification leverages elements such as points, badges, leaderboards, challenges, and rewards to encourage users to interact more deeply with a product or service. Here are few gamification elements to learn and use in Designs:

CHAPTER 14
Gamification in UX Design

"Time or item running out.
Items in limited supply are often perceived as more valuable by people."

Introduction

A very popular word in design, product, and business discussions, nowadays. People expect the designer to gamify a certain flow or screen, and the expectations remain around making it colorful, having some interaction, or having some reward mechanism. However, I want to convey that gamification is much more than that.

Gamification refers to the application of game-design elements and principles in non-game contexts. This technique is used to enhance user engagement, organizational productivity, learning, employee recruitment and evaluation, ease of use, usefulness of systems, and physical exercise.

Here are some key aspects of gamification:

- Motivation
- Rewards
- Behavior change
- Learning and education, and so on.

Gamification should be designed carefully to ensure that it promotes positive engagement and does not lead to unintended negative consequences, such as promoting addictive behaviors or prioritizing game-like rewards over real-world values and objectives.

There are a lot of elements of gamification that we must know how to use. We will discuss a few of the elements in subsequent chapters. We will learn:

- Scarcity
- Social Proof
- Reciprocation
- Positive and negative reinforcement
- Shared commitment

We will explore these elements further in detail:

Structure

In this chapter of Gamification, we are going to cover:

- Scarcity
- Social proof
- Reciprocation
- Positive and negative reinforcement
- Shared commitment

Objectives

Gamification is the word originated from the word *game*. In this chapter we will discuss how the logics and attributes of game can help the physical and digital product get more engagement and motivate the users to perform a particular task. Gamification is one of the biggest levers to drive engagement and retention in any of the platform or digital product. There are lot of parts to gamification and in this chapter, we will cover few impactful ones. We will discuss live examples from the real world as well as learnings and how to use those effectively in your digital product. We will discuss about:

- Scarcity
- Social Proof
- Reciprocation
- Positive and negative reinforcement
- Shared commitment

Scarcity

The principle of scarcity, as a key method of persuasion, posits that an item's perceived value increases when its availability is limited. This concept is one of six fundamental principles in the art of persuasion.

The scarcity principle suggests that when an item is marketed as being scarce or available for a limited duration, consumers are more likely to make a purchase. The perception of rarity or time-limited availability often prompts people to act quickly to acquire the item in question.

This is a layer of persuasive design in UX that will add a lot of value to your decision-making process. After this chapter, you will be able to persuade your users to complete a particular action.

History and origin of scarcity

The scarcity principle, as a psychological and marketing concept, was not originally or specifically attributed to a single founder or associated with the field of gamification. Instead, it stems from broader psychological and economic principles that have been observed and studied over time.

In the realm of psychology, the concept of scarcity affecting human behavior has been extensively explored by *Robert Cialdini*, particularly in his 1984 book, *Influence: The Psychology of Persuasion*. *Cialdini* identified scarcity as one of the key principles of influence, noting that people are more likely to desire something that they perceive as scarce or in limited supply.

However, the application of the scarcity principle in gamification is part of a more recent trend where traditional psychological principles are applied to game design to enhance engagement and motivation. This application does not have a single **founder** as such but is rather the result of many game designers and psychologists applying established psychological principles to the context of games and user engagement strategies.

Therefore, while the scarcity principle has been a well-known concept in psychology and economics for a long time, its specific adaptation into gamification is a product of collective development rather than the discovery of an individual.

The scarcity design pattern can be effectively implemented to:

- Accelerate decision-making processes
- Imply the worth or value of a product or service
- Stimulate actions such as buying or other specific behaviors
- Discourage users from spending too much time pondering their decision

When you listen to the word scarcity, what do you relate it to for the very first time? I assume there are few ways to think about it:

- **When the item is going to be out of stock**: This suggests that the availability of this item is becoming increasingly limited. If action is not taken promptly, there is a risk of it being completely sold out. Therefore, it is advisable to act quickly before the item is out of stock. Since there is a risk of an item being unavailable, it is time-based thing. Act before it goes out of stock.

- **When an offer is approaching its expiration:** It seems as though there is a temporary discount or special offer on a product or service. This offer is available only for a short period of time. If we do not act swiftly, we will miss out on this opportunity and will have to purchase it at a higher price later. Hence, it is also a time-based thing. You are running out of time to take quick action.

- **Early access or join waiting list:** It has been noted that restrictions often increase the desire to engage in a particular activity, with exclusivity being particularly appealing. People generally enjoy the privilege of early access to offers or the opportunity to join a waiting list for a product that is out of stock, as this tends to heighten their curiosity and interest.

  The goal of the above scenarios is to push the users to take action quickly before they run out of time or stock. If you do online shopping, travel booking, or a lot of other kinds of transactions, you must have experienced such cases.

- **When the item is going to be out of stock**: Let us look at a few examples from digital media (websites and mobile apps). Refer to *Figure 14.1* which is the product listing pages of Myntra:

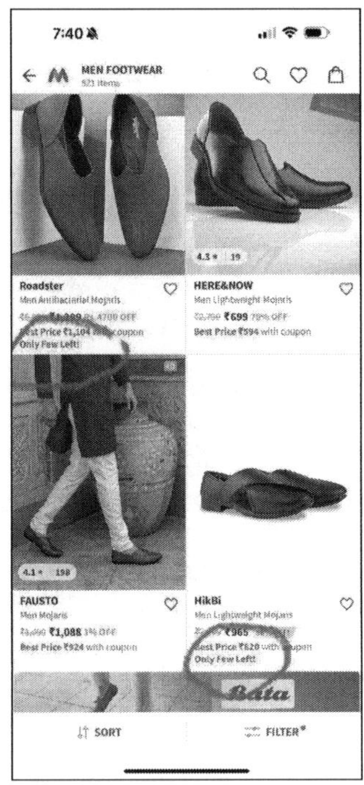

Figure 14.1: *Myntra Product Listing page with Scarcity example*

Refer to *Figure 14.2* which depicts the listing page of Nykaa:

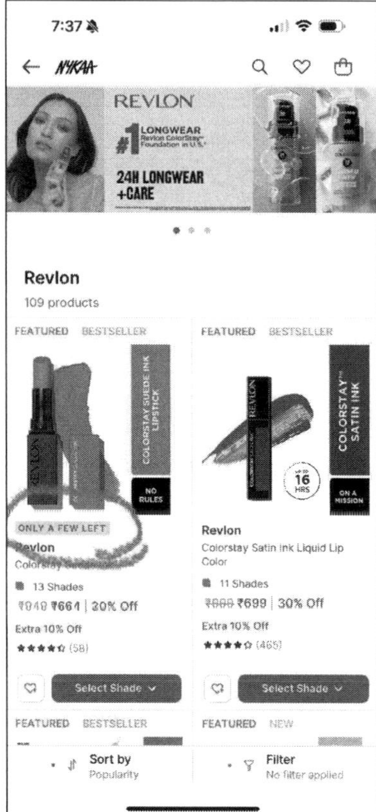

Figure 14.2: Nykaa Product Listing page with Scarcity example

Both are famous e-commerce websites for buying fashion and beauty products. Did you notice how both these figures are highlighting the scarcity effect to generate urgency and sell their products faster? Both highlight the fact that there are only a few products left. They are not giving a number, but this certainly brings some urgency to the user's mind about losing the deal's benefit, if they do not grab the offer right then and there.

- Let us look at another example of Amazon. Referring to *Figure 14.3* which contains the details page of a product at Amazon, they highlight the scarcity of the product by giving an actual number that **Only 1 left in stock**. This brings a sense of urgency in the user's mind of losing this deal if they truly like this product but if they do not react or buy immediately, they might not get this deal. If the user desperately needed the product, they would not want to take a risk and allow someone to buy the only 1 left in stock before them.

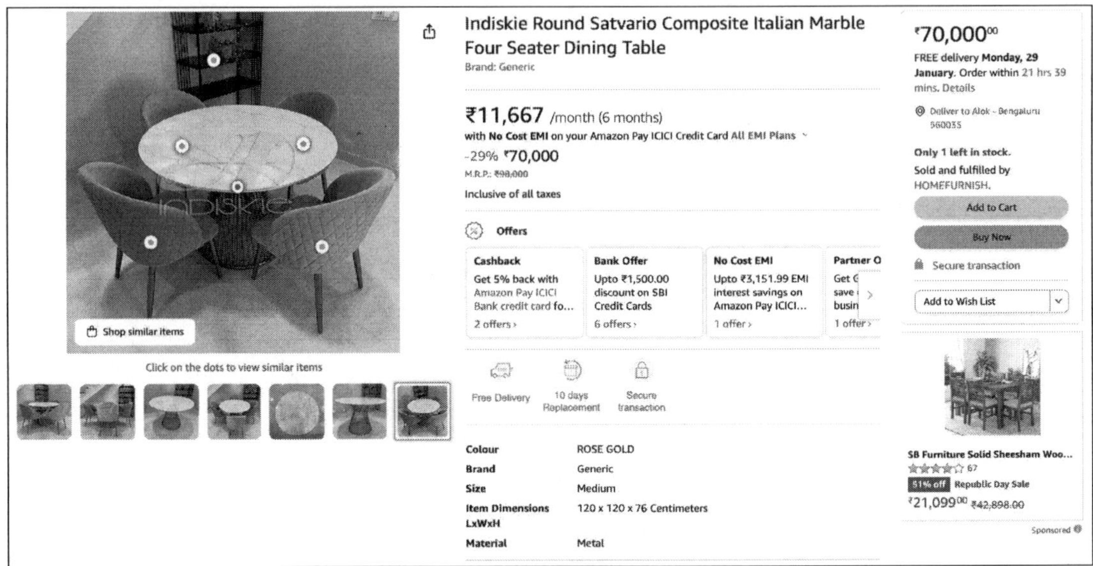

Figure 14.3: Amazon product details page highlights, "Only 1 left in stock."

Now, a point of discussion here is that, are these details factually correct? Is there really 1 piece of the product left in their stock or is it just to create false sense of urgency?

As a brand/platform, it is your responsibility to communicate the right information to gain the trust of your users. Having a false number just to create urgency is unfair to your user. One of the most important parts is that this is a **dark pattern**, and you should avoid it as much as possible. There are many countries where there are government rules and penalties in place to control such patterns used in e-commerce websites:

- **When an offer is approaching its expiration**: Let us observe the example around us when time is crucial or there are some offer for limited time only. E-commerce websites inform the users about the sale/offer ending soon, whether it be a particular date or time (refer to the following figure):

The preceding *Figure 14.4* is a screen of Amazon, and it is when Amazon's Great Republic Day sale is live. Amazon highlights some special prices and special launches during the sale and decides to highlight the sale's ending time when it is approaching it is expiration time.

Figure 14.4: *Amazon highlights Sale ending date with running timer*

This direction creates urgency within the user, so in-case I do not buy it immediately or within the same time, I am not going to get this offer after a certain time.

Now let us look at the MakeMyTrip website (a well-known travel booking website in India). Refer to *Figure 14.5*; it is the deals page, and it has all the offers. You will notice they are running a timer in the black highlighted box that conveys that particular deal/offer MakeMyTrip is promoting a sense of urgency to take a decision if you really like this deal because it is going to end very soon. This kind of information drives the conversion of users. They end up buying the deal before it ends because the price might look lucrative.

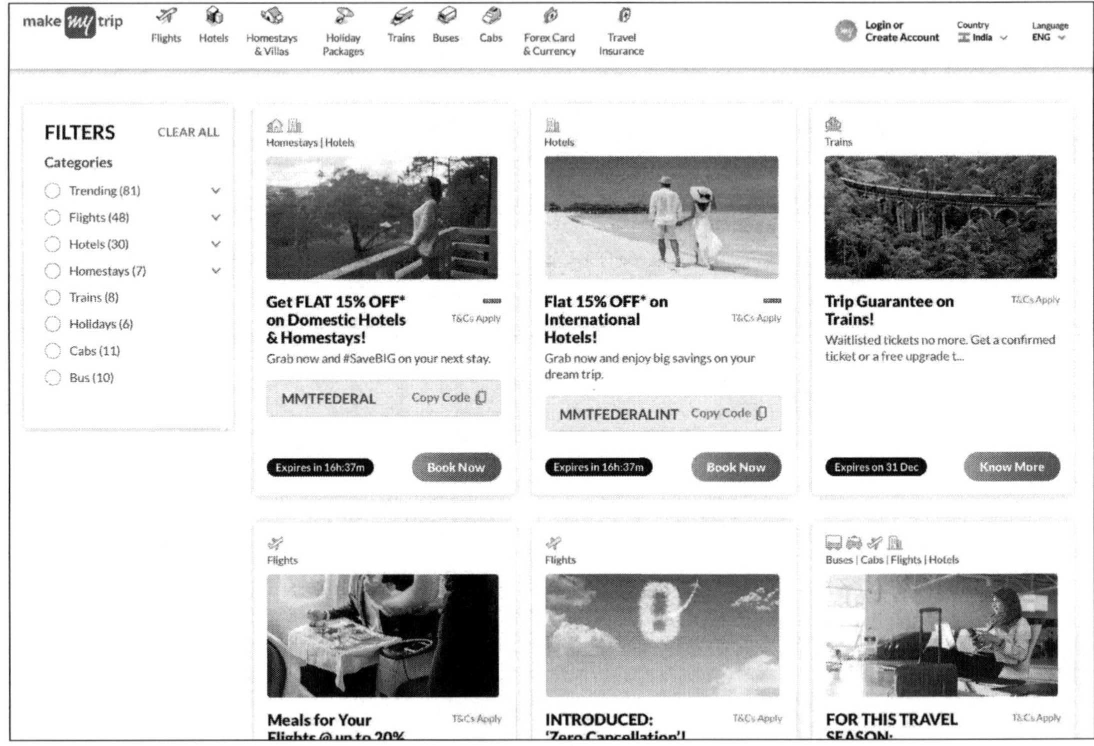

Figure 14.5: MakeMyTrip Holiday package page with Expiring deals

The point to note here is that you should not create a false urgency with a falsely expiring offer and then resetting the timer after expiration. It is a trust issue as well as the Dark Pattern. Please ignore the dark patterns.

- **Early access or join waiting list**: Numerous compelling studies demonstrate that imposing restrictions on something can increase people's interest. For instance, if a feature is made available for unlimited use, it often goes unnoticed or unused. However, if you limit its use to only three times a day, you will frequently observe a surge in enthusiasm as people eagerly utilize their limited usage rights and often strive to unlock a fourth opportunity.

Remember when ChatGPT and a lot of other AI tools were launched, and you wanted to explore the tool before anyone else. A lot of tools had a waiting period because of heavy demand, and it was a great way to create the scarcity effect and spread curiosity. Since it was not available for everyone, people applied to wait. Whoever got the tool first had a sense of achievement and the rest continued to start waiting for the tool. Refer to the following *Figure 14.6*; it is the ChatGPT upgrade screen. ChatGPT Plus which is the paid upgrade was not available for everyone at a certain time, and this situation gave it more virality:

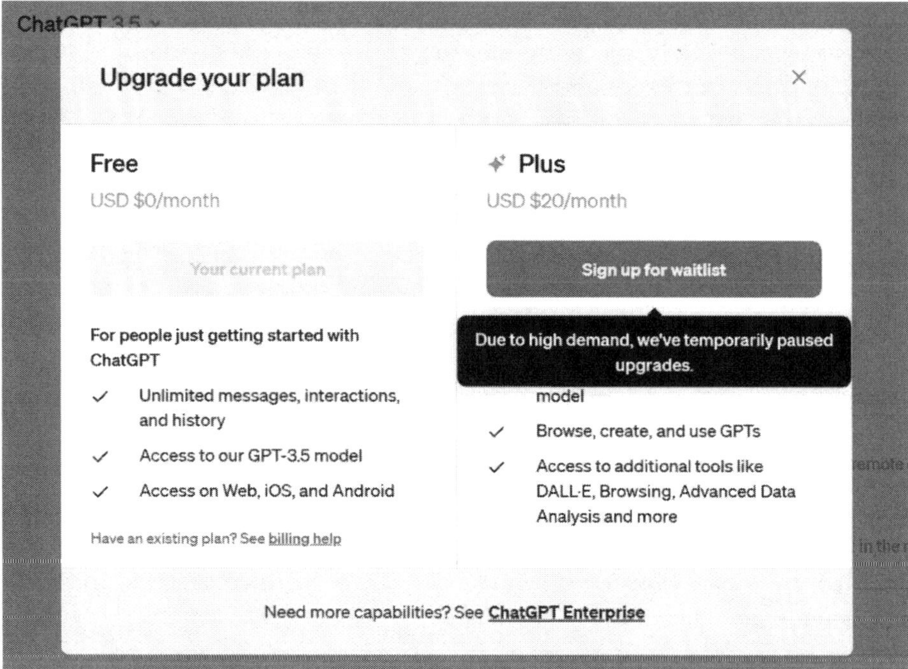

Figure 14.6: *ChatGPT Plus upgrade screen*

Another beautiful example is Myntra's End of Reason Sale. They always give early access to their privileged Insider members. That gives it virality among the users who then aim to become Insiders so that they also get access before everyone else. Referring to *Figure 14.7*, it is a banner on their website when they announce the sale with early access to insiders, and it creates scarcity and a feeling of exclusivity for the users, which they eventually buy during the sale. They also start to figure out how to become insiders as that gives them additional benefits.

Figure 14.7: *Myntra sale stats only for premium insider customers*

Scarcity is a very interesting principle of gamification to drive engagement and conversion, but it needs to be used wisely and with integrity, or else you may end up following a dark pattern. So be fair to your users and use this method to convey the right information to them at the right time.

Key takeaways

- **Enhanced perceived value:** In gamification, implementing scarcity can significantly raise the perceived value of a product or feature. When something is scarce or available for a limited time, it becomes more desirable to users, leading them to value it more highly.

- **Increased user engagement:** Scarcity can drive users to engage more frequently with a product. For instance, if a game offers a rare item for a limited period, players are more likely to log in regularly or perform specific actions to obtain it.

- **Urgency-driven actions:** Scarcity creates a sense of urgency, prompting users to act quickly. This is particularly effective in decision-making scenarios where users might otherwise delay or be indecisive. By introducing time-limited offers or exclusive access, users are motivated to take immediate action.

- **Exclusivity and status:** Scarcity can instill a sense of exclusivity and status among users. Owning or achieving something rare within a game can offer bragging rights and a feeling of accomplishment, which enhances the overall user experience.

- **Balancing challenge and accessibility:** While scarcity can be a powerful tool, it is important to balance it carefully to ensure that it does not lead to frustration or disengagement. If users feel that rare items or features are unattainably scarce, it might lead to a negative experience. Effective gamification through scarcity involves making these items challenging but still achievable to maintain user interest and satisfaction.

So, let us conclude this section. Scarcity is a very interesting and important element of gamification. If it is rightly used, it is very helpful for the users. It helps them not to miss any important offers or products. With the help of all the scarcity techniques, users are motivated to take quick action and complete the step that really is needed for them.

We should not misuse this technique to pass false information and should not create false urgency. This leads to a dark pattern of UX, and for this, a lot of countries have rules and penalties. Hence, take precautions while using scarcity. Use it well; do not misuse it.

We are done with our first chapter of gamification. I hope you will be able to use it in your next product to motivate your users. In the next chapter, we are going to discuss about the Social Proof; another gamification element that motivates the users to take action quickly.

Social proof

Social proof is a psychological phenomenon where individuals look to others' actions to inform their own decisions. This behavior stems from our inherent desire to act **correctly** in various situations, including making purchases, choosing dining locations, deciding where to go, and determining our interactions. A prime real-life illustration of social proof is the long queue outside an Apple Store on the launch day of a new iPhone. The sight of people eagerly waiting, sometimes for hours, influences our perception of the phone's worth and often increases our own desire for it.

History and origin of social proof

Social proof is a key concept among the six principles of influence outlined in *Dr. Robert Cialdini's Influence: The Psychology of Persuasion*, first published in 1984. As a psychology professor, *Cialdini*, with his students, conducted extensive research to validate these principles. Social proof capitalizes on our uncertainties and the innate desire to make the *right* decision.

In usability studies, it is not uncommon to encounter users who claim indifference to user reviews, express distrust in others' opinions, and rely solely on their own judgment. However, a multitude of psychological studies debunk this notion of the **lone wolf** approach, demonstrating its inaccuracy. This disparity underscores the importance of designing based on users' actions rather than their stated preferences.

Studies in social psychology have consistently shown our deep-rooted, often subconscious, dependence on others' behavior to guide our own decision-making processes. A prevalent example of social proof in action is the widely criticized use of laugh tracks in sitcoms. *Cialdini* observes that laugh tracks lead audiences to laugh longer and more frequently at comedic content and to perceive the content as funnier, especially for weaker jokes.

Social proof is a psychological concept where individuals mimic the actions of others, perceiving them as the appropriate response to a specific situation

— Robert Cialdini

In a human context, have you ever noticed that we notice each other's actions and behaviors a lot? Being observers, we are easily influenced by someone narrating their success story, and that makes us want to be like them. We are influenced by someone's lifestyle, way of working, health, wealth, and so on. That is human nature. We tend to want to learn from someone superior to us, changing our own actions and behaviors accordingly.

In the earlier context, society meant the people around us, our family and friends, a few acquaintances, and so on, however now, because of internet penetration and the vast usage of social media, we are past that limited illusion. The vast virtual society, that is social media, and the world of the internet is also society.

Before social media, people would get influenced by society, which only meant their near and dear people, but now you have a complete world to get inspiration from. You may follow a leader of your field or choice or a famous personality on the web these days and you may get to know a lot about them, their habits, their lifestyle, and so on. For social media influencers, their job is to influence you. People following them, learn from their behavior and the products or lifestyle they endorse. That is what is social proof.

Social proof represents external endorsements indicating the trustworthiness and value of a product or service. Forms of social proof encompass:

- Customer testimonials and user feedback,
- Detailed case studies,
- Recognitions, awards, and certifications,
- Media coverage, press features, and so on.

We will discuss a few of these elements in subsequent pages. Let us understand the most important one first, which is testimonials and feedback.

Customer testimonials and user feedback

Do you shop online, and do you check customer reviews and ratings before you shortlist or buy a product?

This is normal behavior for shoppers these days, online. I have observed via data and a lot of my user research that the user shortlists items as per brand, price, and details they are looking for, but immediately after this information, users want to see another user's review and rating.

People do check the reviews to build some trust in the product, and they want to know the experience of other users with the product. These are the biggest drivers for buying a product. Refer to *Figure 14.8* and notice how Amazon highlights the rating of every product, rated by the user who has already bought it. It also reflects the number of users who rated. This is a great example of social proof. People do trust other people's experiences, and they take their decisions as per their activities. It builds trust in a particular product and since ratings build trust, Amazon gives you options to compare a few similar products, highlighting the rating of the specific feature/USP of the product. (refer to *Figure 14.8*)

Figure 14.8: Amazon highlights the rating and the number of users who rated

Moreover, many users filter their search results as per a certain rating, like, *show me results/ products* that have a minimum a four-star rating out of five (refer to the following figure):

Figure 14.9: Amazon highlights the comparison of products by rating

Have a look at *Figure 14.10* and *Figure 14.11*. The e-commerce portals now have the option to filter items according to their ratings. Judging by this user behavior, it is a promising feature to build trust and help them narrow their search results.

Figure 14.10: Amazon filter by rating

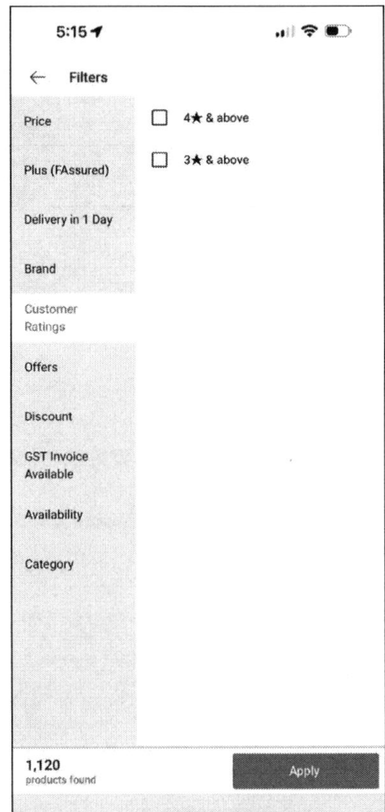

Figure 14.11: Myntra filter by rating

Ratings are quantitative numbers that validate and build trust between the site and the user. There is another need for users to know the qualitative feedback of a product, which is the product review section, that most of the e-commerce has now.

Refer to *Figure 14.12*, showing the product detail page on Amazon, and the Customer Review section, where users can write the complete details about a product, including pros and cons with ratings. It highlights an important element that relates to the product, like, quality, value, and appearance, as a positive part, and a few negative parts, like weight and size.

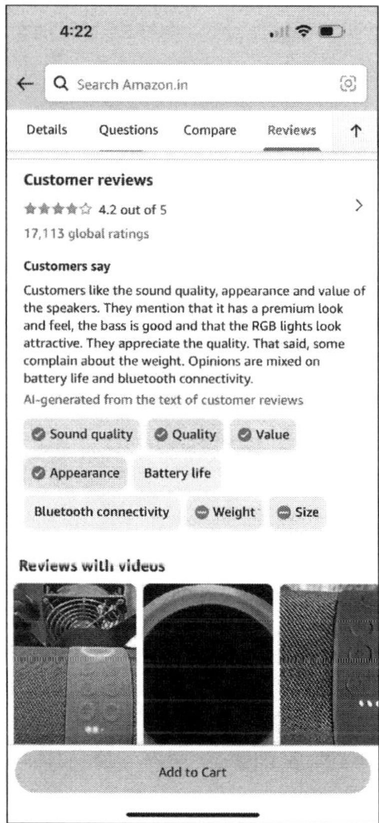

Figure 14.12: *Amazon shares customer review of the product*

Refer to *Figure 14.13*, the product detail page on Myntra, with the **Ratings** and **Reviews** sections combined. You will notice it highlights the specific part's ratings by user, like Fit, length in terms of tight, loose, and so on. This gives an extra layer of deep understanding about the product that builds more trust in the specifications of the product. They are also given an option to showcase pictures. The following figure contains real pictures that were uploaded by users after wearing the same apparel. It makes the users trust the platform more, checking out normal users like them wearing it because till now they have seen these apparel worn by models who are supposed to look attractive by looks, while being aware that the images are edited. But when it is seen on normal users like us, it builds more trust in the user's mind.

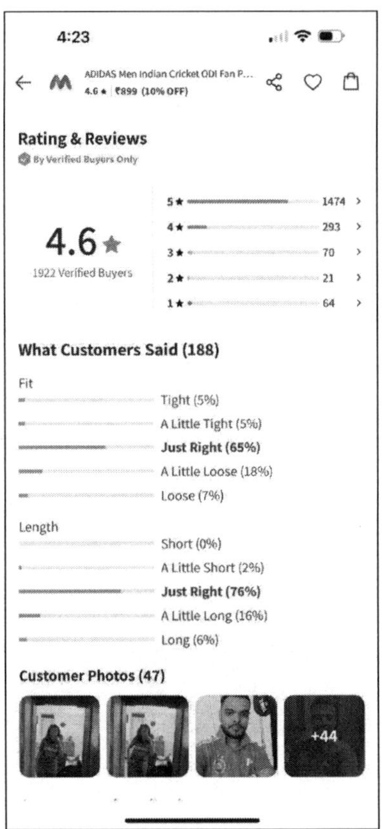

Figure 14.13: Myntra shares a Review of the product with images

Do you think this works only in the e-commerce world?

Social proof is an important aspect in a lot of other fields. For example, let us have a look at *Figure 14.14,* which is from LinkedIn (a social media for professionals). When you search for someone on LinkedIn and select the profile, it will show the details about the person and their professional activities. However, did you notice a section at the right side, which is **People also viewed?** This section is social proof to drive more engagement on the platform that you should check out these similar profiles as well which is being seen by other people. If you do not click these or connect with them, it feels like you are missing out on something. This builds trust between the platform and the user, which helps you connect with like-minded folks who could be a relevant and useful connection to the user. It is a recommendation by the platform to engage you.

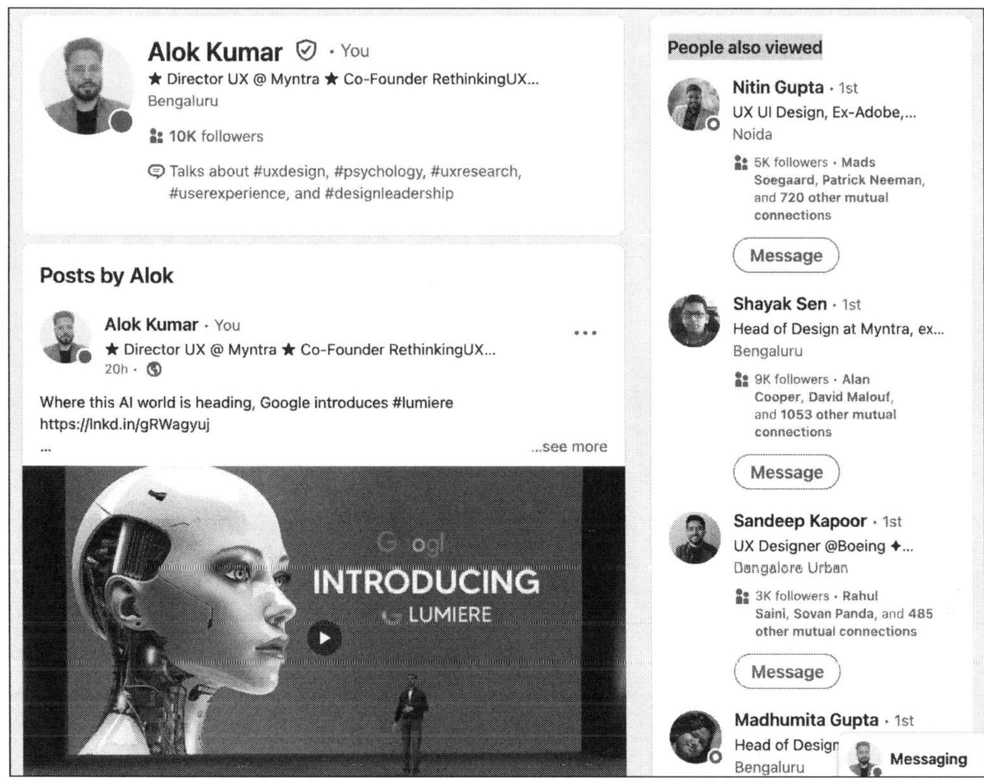

Figure 14.14: *LinkedIn highlights people who also viewed sections)*

Now let us discuss another aspect of social proof, which is recognition and awards. Have you noticed that a lot of companies highlight their achievements, like the list of their clients? For example, refer to *Figure 14.15*, which is from a design agency, they highlight their list of clients to build more trust with visiting and new clients.

Figure 14.15: *List of clients of an agency (Service provider)*

This list of clients showcased on the website helps the brands gain more trust and visibility. The better the client list, the bigger the trust.

Another way of using social proof is to showcase achievements, rewards, and recognition to the world and gain more trust and visibility. For example, refer to *Figure 14.16*. These are the awards and achievements of a particular design agency, and they highlighted all their awards and achievements on their website. This makes them get the trust of new clients who are coming to them for design solutions. This act of social proof is very helpful because most of the brands do highlight their achievements on their website as well as social media.

Figure 14.16: List of achievements and awards by an agency

Key takeaways of how to use social proof

- Here are the key takeaways from this section. Host social media takeovers by industry experts.
- Express gratitude for social mentions.
- Celebrate and publicize achievements, badges, and verifications.
- Consider appointing brand ambassadors.

- Compile and showcase content created by users.
- Broadcast your customers' enthusiasm for your products.
- Feature customer testimonials prominently on your website.
- Highlight the magnitude of your customer base in your profile bio.
- Motivate customers to post positive reviews on your social platforms.
- Exhibit the count of social media shares.

So, now let us conclude this section.

Social proof is another key element of gamification that helps build trust. As we discussed in the chapter, people do need people's opinions, especially when it comes to buying a product.

Social proof helps us validate our actions if we are making a good decision (while buying stuff online) which also helps us change our actions as per the feedback and experience shared by others.

Since the definition of society has become very broad after the penetration of the internet and social media, people tend to take the opinions of others and get influenced by the endorsements of any celebrity or leader.

I hope you will use social proof in your next product to build the trust of the users and convert that into conversion and retention of your product.

In the next chapter, we are going to explore another important aspect of gamification, which is Reciprocation. Reciprocation teaches us to motivate the user by giving them some reward first and then expecting back from them. We will discuss their motivation theory in a deep manner with examples.

Reciprocation

Reciprocity is a social principle, that is also part of persuasive design. It involves returning positive gestures with similar acts, thus encouraging kindness. When applied to any digital product experience. This means users are inclined to interact more with a product that initially offers them value. This also builds trust and increases the likelihood of them giving back to the product via completing an action or buying on platform. This principle becomes particularly crucial when requesting significant actions from users, such as signing up or encountering a paywall.

In short, when you are offered something for free or as a positive gesture, it is highly likely that you will be obliged to give back in some form which we will be discussing further in this section.

History and origin of reciprocation

The principle of reciprocation in psychology was not discovered by a single individual but rather has been a part of human social behavior for a long time. In this *Cialdini's* book, he identified reciprocation as one of the six key principles of influence. He explored how the norm of reciprocity operates as a powerful driver of human behavior, compelling individuals to return favors or kindnesses.

The adoption of the principle of reciprocation in design, particularly in the fields of user experience and interaction design, is more of a collective evolution than the discovery of a single individual. Designers and researchers in the UX field began incorporating principles from psychology, including reciprocation, to better understand and predict user behaviors and to create more engaging and effective designs. This interdisciplinary approach has been a hallmark of the UX design field, where insights from psychology are regularly integrated into design practices.

> *The rule for reciprocation says that we should try to repay, in kind,*
> *what another person has provided us.*
>
> — *Robert Cialdini*

The concept of reciprocity suggests a natural inclination in humans to repay favors, as people generally dislike feeling indebted to others. This instinct is deeply rooted in our nature as social creatures, a trait fundamental to the evolution and success of humankind. It is as if we are innately programmed to sustain the social dynamics that have enabled our species to thrive.

This powerful impulse can, unfortunately, make people susceptible to manipulative tactics used by con artists. However, it can also be harnessed positively to build relationships, which is particularly beneficial for online businesses. Offering something for free, like a trial, valuable content, or a complimentary service, can be an effective way to engage customers.

In the realm of getting more business via online, **Search Engine Optimization (SEO)** or social media help, this principle is equally potent. Exchanging valuable offerings for a prospect's email can be quite straightforward, provided that the value is significant and communicated effectively.

Let us explore how reciprocation has been used in history and its validity in current scenarios:

- **Social psychology roots:** The principle of reciprocation is deeply rooted in social psychology. It was popularized as Cialdini's 1984 book, *Influence: The Psychology of Persuasion*. He identified reciprocation as one of the key principles of influence, describing it as a powerful social norm where people feel compelled to return favors or kindness.

- **Early application in marketing and advertising:** Before its widespread adoption in UX design, the principle of reciprocation was used in marketing and advertising. Businesses would provide something of value for free (like samples or gifts) with the expectation that recipients would feel a social obligation to reciprocate, often in the form of a purchase.

- **Shift to digital design:** With the advent of the internet and digital products, the concept of reciprocation began to be applied in web design and user experience. Websites started to offer valuable content or services for free, such as useful articles, free trials, or software demos, anticipating that users would reciprocate with their loyalty, continued usage, or purchases.

- **User Experience (UX) design:** In UX design, reciprocation is used to create positive user experiences that encourage continued engagement and loyalty. For example, if a website provides a user-friendly experience or valuable content, users may be more inclined to sign up for a newsletter, make a purchase, or recommend the site to others.

- **Gamification and loyalty programs:** The principle of reciprocation has also been employed in gamification strategies and loyalty programs within apps and websites. Users receive rewards, points, or benefits in return for their engagement or purchases, fostering a cycle of ongoing interaction.

- **Ethical considerations:** As the application of reciprocation in design has grown, so have the discussions about its ethical implications. Designers and companies are increasingly aware of the importance of using this principle responsibly, ensuring that it does not manipulate or exploit users.

- **Current trends:** In contemporary design, especially with the focus on user-centered design, reciprocation is seen as a way to build trust and a positive relationship with users. It is about creating a mutual value exchange where both parties benefit—the user receives something of value, and the business gains engagement, loyalty, or sales.

Now let us explore how reciprocity is being used in the digital medium with some examples:

Look at the following *Figure 14.17*, *Figure 14.18*, and *Figure 14.19*. Did you notice that brands like Spotify, LinkedIn, and Netflix provide their free trial for a certain period and do not ask for any money during that time (some places these platforms ask for your credit card info only but do not charge you). Additionally, they give you the option to cancel it anytime you wish without getting charged extra during trial period.

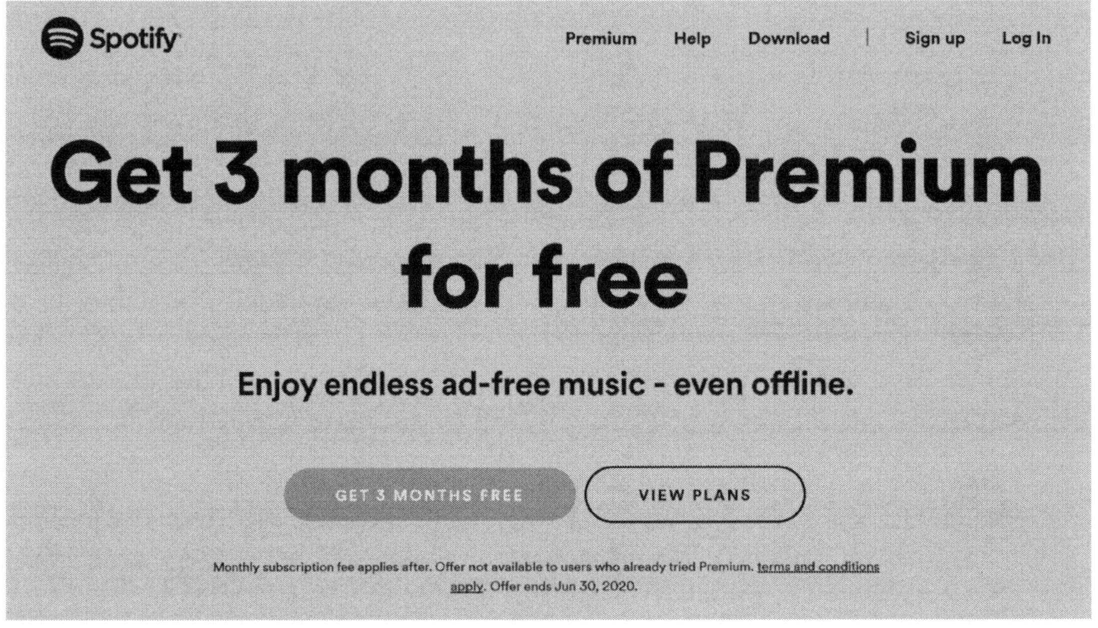

Figure 14.17: *3 months free trial of Spotify premium*

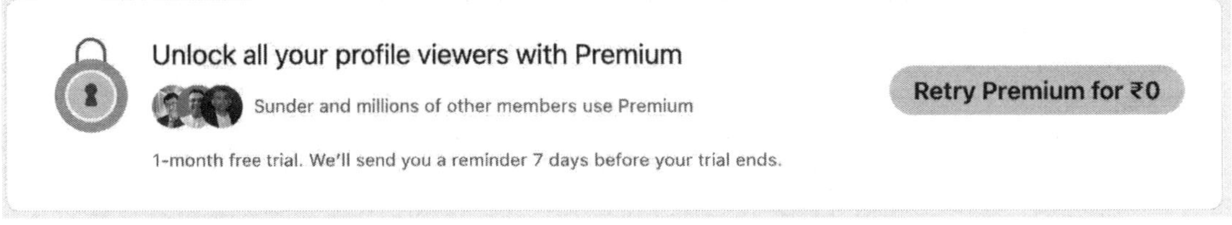

Figure 14.18: *1-month free trial of LinkedIn premium*

Figure 14.19: *1-month free subscription of Netflix*

In fact, they do highlight these options promptly on their homepage. For example, refer to *Figure 14.20*. By highlighting **Cancel anytime**, these brands build the user's trust as well.

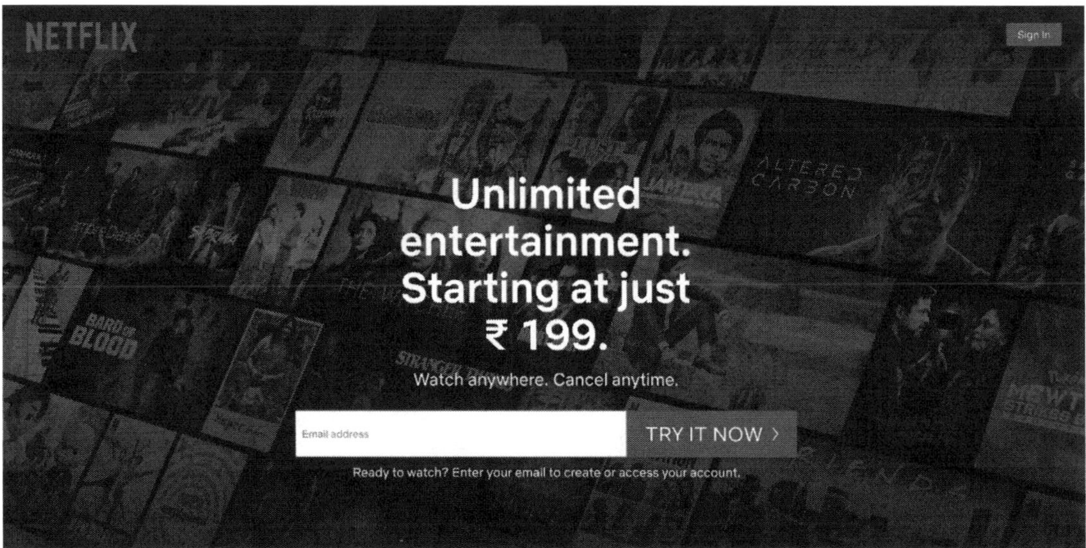

Figure 14.20: Netflix highlights on their homepage that you may cancel anytime.

Why do these brands provide a free trial of their products for a certain time? This is what the reciprocation effect entails. Since you have used the product for some time, it is very likely that you might want to continue and pay for a paid subscription. Of course, not everyone subscribes, but a good number of users do. At this point in time, there are two kinds of gamification logic being applied.

One is reciprocation, because as humans we have a tendency to give back, and since we used a service for free for some time, we are likely to convert to becoming a paid user.

Another gamification logic is **habit building**. You had never used the product, but since it was free for some time, you subscribed to their free trial for a period of time. And while using the product for some time, you figured out some useful features and use cases that fulfill your requirements, and you found it useful. Now that it is worth using, you build a habit of using the product and end up buying the subscription after the end of your free trial.

Reciprocation has been used a lot in games too, where you are offered some reward for free or by doing some easy activity, and after you receive the reward, you are expected to complete a particular task, so that engagement on their platform goes up. High engagement consequentially has a high probability of conversion (as a paid user / player), so players end up buying some pack or plans. Few games will immediately pitch a particular pack of game currency to continue the game and those offers would be like such a beneficial offer that you would want to opt for it.

Let us look at examples from games where reciprocation is applied. Have a look at *Figure 14.21*, it is a screen of the Coin Master game. One of the most famous and addictive Chinese mobile games. When you login to the game every day, you are provided with a Daily bonus. On this screen they may give you a Valentine 's Day bonus because if it is February, which they would be promoting, trying to be relevant to the time.

Figure 14.21: Coin Master Daily Bonus collection

If you notice this preceding screen, when they give you a daily bonus, it is a reward for you for free and you are not supposed to buy anything else, no need to spend money at all. Do you think a user will ever say NO to such an offer? Of course not. Players end up accepting these rewards, and just imagine what is the expectation of the game from the players. They want players to play and not run out of their coins/currency. They have a lot of other mechanisms to sink the coin that you got, and when you spend some time playing and your daily reward coins are also over, you look for more coins, you may end up buying a coin pack to continue the game.

In the case of *Figure 14.21*, the game does not ask you to spend immediately but may ask later.

Now have a look at another example from the same game in *Figure 14.22*. Here, there are multiple cases. The game is providing you with some free currency, but it is locked, and you are expected to perform a few activities to unlock this free reward for you. You may end up performing a small activity to get this free reward. At the same time, they are trying to sell you another exciting game like Currency Pack, which might look like a deal you must grab. In this second case, the reciprocity is handled in such a manner that you are being given some free reward, but for that, you are supposed to do some small activity as well as try to upsell immediately on the same screen.

Figure 14.22: Coin Master welcome treat / gift

Another very good example of reciprocation in our day to day lives is social media. In today's world, I observe many people active on social media. They are either making content (as a content creator) or are consumers who consume all the information via social media posts, reels, shorts, and so on. Refer to *Figure 14.23* (social media posts with likes and comments number).

Figure 14.23: Social media posts with likes and comments

The consumer's motivation is to see interesting content for the purpose of entertainment as well as interesting insights and information, and they end up spending hours and hours on social media platforms.

However, what is the motivation of these content creators, who are very actively creating a lot of content for consumers? Do you realize how much of their own bandwidth they spend creating that content?

Do you see the reciprocation here??

The content creators' expectations are to get more views, likes, shares, and subscriptions from the content consumers. They do share the content for free with the people and via reciprocity logic, they end up getting likes, shares, and so on.

Key takeaways

- It enhances user engagement
- It facilitates user acquisition
- The probability of conversion goes up
- It helps build trust because you provide something for free
- Increases perceived value

In summary, reciprocity in design is about creating a mutual value exchange between the product and its users, leading to trust, engagement, loyalty, and an overall better UX.

The principle of reciprocity is a fundamental aspect of human interactions and is crucial in the realm of digital product design.

By integrating the concept of reciprocity, designers are able to craft user experiences that transcend user engagement, acquisition, retention while also driving the trust and perceived value of your product.

Utilizing tactics such as free trials, daily bonuses, unexpected rewards, active social media engagement, encouraging user-generated content, and incorporating elements of gamification, designers can build deeper connections with users and nurture their loyalty.

Therefore, let us harness the power of reciprocity in our design approaches to develop digital products that genuinely connect with users and create a profound and enduring effect.

Keep in mind that in digital product design, even a small gesture of reciprocity can make a significant difference!

In the next section, we are going to deep dive into another important aspect of gamification, which is reinforcement. Reinforcement drives the engagement of the users, and depending on the scenarios and the users, we must use both positive and negative reinforcement.

We will discuss how to reinforce positively and negatively at certain points in time and achieve better user engagement.

Reinforcement

In design, the term **reinforcement** refers to the concept of strengthening or emphasizing certain elements within a design to support the overall message, functionality, or aesthetic. This can be achieved through various means, depending on the context of the design.

Reinforcement in design is about strategically using design elements and principles to bolster the effectiveness and coherence of the design, whether it is in terms of visual appeal, functionality, message delivery, or structural integrity.

History and origin of reinforcement

Reinforcement theory, particularly as it is applied in the context of psychology and behavior, is most often associated with *B.F. Skinner* and his work in the field of behaviorism. However, when we talk about **reinforcement** in the context of design, we are generally referring to principles that are not directly attributable to a single discoverer or seminal moment, but rather to a broader evolution of design principles over time.

In design, the concept of reinforcement relates to emphasizing certain elements to strengthen the overall message, functionality, or aesthetic of a design. This concept has been an integral part of design practice across various disciplines (like graphic design, industrial design, architecture, and UX design) and has evolved naturally as part of the design profession's growth and adaptation to new challenges and technologies.

So, while *B.F. Skinner's* reinforcement theory is a specific psychological concept describing how behavior can be shaped by rewards and punishments, the use of reinforcement in design is a proven and great practice that do not have a single point of origin or discovery. It is accurate to say that these principles have developed organically within the design field over time.

The history of reinforcement in design is not a singular narrative but a collection of developments across various fields of design, including architecture, graphic design, industrial design, and user experience design. Reinforcement as a principle has been intrinsic to design since its inception, evolving with each field's history. It affects a lot of vertices, for example, architecture, graphic design, industrial design, user experience design, sustainability in design, etc.

User Experience Design is a relatively new field that emerged with the advent of digital interfaces. Reinforcement in UX design involves guiding and affirming user actions and decisions, ensuring intuitive and efficient interaction with products. This aspect of design has evolved rapidly with the digital revolution, as understanding of user behavior and technology has advanced.

The rule for reciprocation says that we should try to repay, in kind, what another person has provided us.

Reinforcement, a term from psychology, refers to stimuli that enhance or increase the likelihood of a particular response. In this dynamic, there are two key players: the reinforcer and the respondent (the individual responding).

Consider a simple illustration involving training a dog. When we want the dog to obey a command, we might use treats as an incentive. Consequently, the dog begins to associate obeying commands with the reward of treats, thereby increasing the likelihood of following future commands.

Another real-life example is academic achievement. If we score high marks in an exam, we are often praised and rewarded by our parents, accompanied by words of encouragement like *good job*. Such rewards and recognition make it more likely that we will strive to repeat this successful behavior in the future.

There are three types of reinforcement, or, as we may say, two ways to motivate the users:

- Positive reinforcement
- Negative reinforcement
- Partial reinforcement

Positive reinforcement

Positive reinforcement involves introducing a stimulus to enhance a response. This concept harks back to the renowned experiment in behavioral psychology involving Pavlov's dog. Pavlov, who introduced the term **reinforcement**, successfully conditioned dogs to salivate at the sound of a bell. By associating the bell with rewards, he established a habitual response (salivation) in the dogs. Praise and rewards are typical forms of positive reinforcement, familiar experiences for many of us, both as providers and recipients.

In the realm of user experience design, positive reinforcement can be applied in two distinct ways. First, for unconventional design elements such as non-standard navigation or unique architectural choices, positive reinforcement can be used to train users. By rewarding their interactions, users are encouraged to become proficient in using these features.

Second, a more common approach is to integrate positive reinforcement across the platform. This method is not about shaping specific behaviors or habits, but rather about promoting continuous and frequent usage of the website or mobile app.

To implement this, focus on the fundamental interactions within your platform. Aim to reward users for completing key actions, thereby fostering a more engaging and enjoyable user experience.

Let us have a look at how positive reinforcement can be used in user experience design.

In the current market, there is a plethora of apps that are strikingly similar in terms of their ultimate goals, information architecture, user interfaces, and target users, making them nearly indistinguishable from each other. So, what strategies can you employ to either compete effectively or launch a superior product?

The answer may lie in user experience.

Consider this common scenario: after filling out lengthy forms and clicking **Submit**, users are often left staring at a blank page, unsure if their submission was successful. Contrast this with a scenario where, instead of a blank page, users are greeted with a simple message like, *Thank you for submitting! We are processing your data.* This small change can significantly alter the user's perception of the process.

Imagine you are making a payment, and after entering the OTP or final payment button, if your screen goes black and you are still waiting for the confirmation, how do you feel? Is it not a frustrating and an anxiety-inducing experience?

Let me show you a sequence of screens when a user tries to make a payment at Cred (an app for paying credit card bill in India). Cred is one of the famous apps in India that is being used to make the payment of credit card bills in India. When a user pays the credit card bill via cred, the interaction of the screens went as per *Figure 14.24, Figure 14.25, Figure 14.26* and *Figure 14.27*.

Figure 14.24: Payment on Cred

Figure 14.25*: Cred Payment (contd.)*

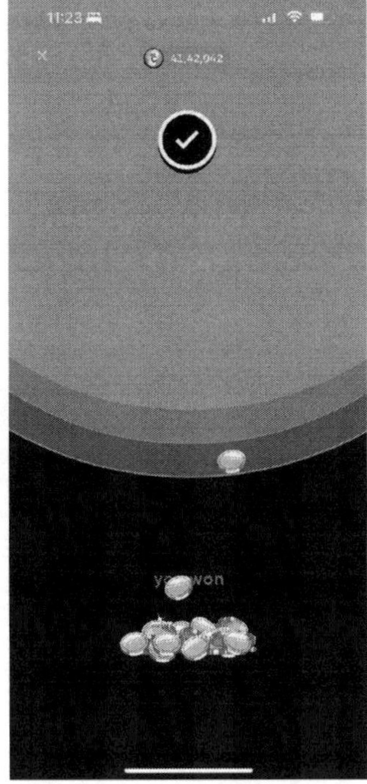

Figure 14.26*: Cred Payment (contd.)*

Figure 14.27*: Payments of Cred*

If you notice how they have engaged with the user. They first conveyed that completing your payment (*Figure 14.24*) and then a tick mark, visual confirmation in *Figure 14.25* and when they confirmed the payment, they also engaged you with some extra reward as coin and cashback.

Such clear, direct messages provide concise confirmations, keeping the user informed about the status of their interactions. Employing this method of positive reinforcement can greatly enhance the overall user experience, making it a key differentiator in a crowded market.

Another example is making the user feel special by giving them some reward once they complete and act or promise them a condition. If you complete this task, you will get this reward. This act increases the participation of the users.

For example, have a look at *Figure 14.28*. It is a screenshot of an online classroom, and this leaderboard appears when a user completes a particular task or answers a quiz in the classroom. The students immediately see a result, with a leaderboard highlighting who gave the right answer and who is in which position in the classroom.

Also at the bottom, the student's personal status is highlighted, so on the current screen, the student got the 7th rank in the class, and this tool is giving him a reason to celebrate and brag about this achievement. Highlighting this achievement itself is a big reward for the students because they want to contribute more to stay at the top of the class leaderboard. This is a classic example of getting more engagement through positive reinforcement.

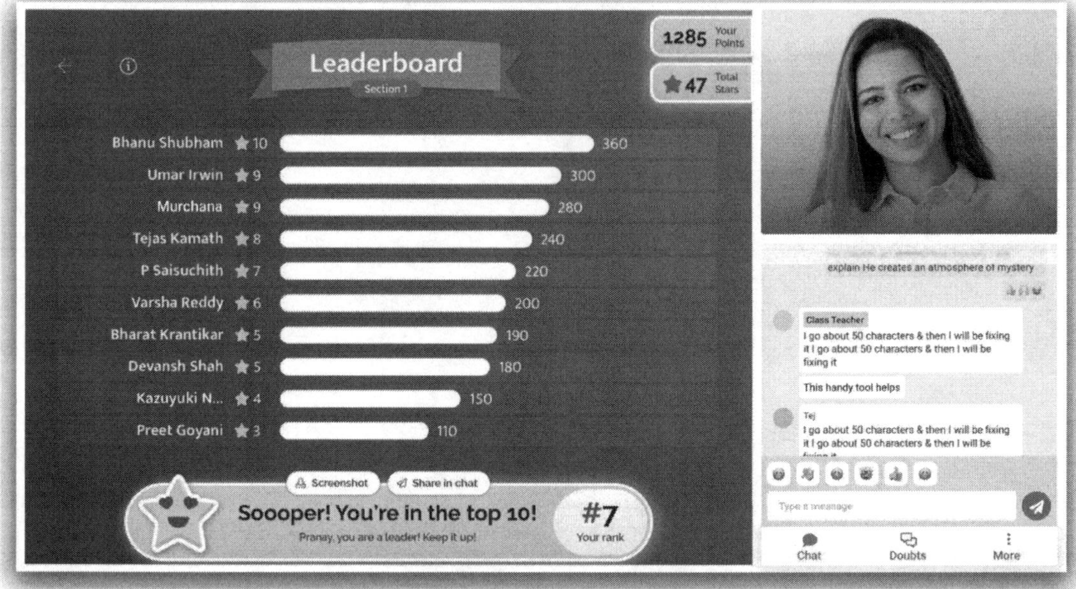

Figure 14.28: Leaderboard of an Online Classroom

Extending to the previous scenario, if the user, who is a student here, gets a reward when he/completes a certain task or the homework, and if this reward was already communicated and promised earlier. It is highly likely that students would want to complete their homework to achieve this badge of Superman/Speedykid and additionally (Refer to *Figure 14.29*), they will earn 60 XP as reward. Such positive reinforcements are famous in the industry to get better engagement.

Figure 14.29: Reward after completing a task

Negative reinforcement

A behavior that increases when a certain stimulus is removed under similar conditions is a response. In this situation, the stimulus functions as negative reinforcement. Or, in a simple term, we may say that if a user is afraid of losing something, it could be his/her achievement or something that completely belongs to you. For example, in the above figure only, which is *Figure 14.29*. It is a screen where you can see the use of positive reinforcement to motivate the students to perform better in the class and achieve a particular badge, which is the speedykid badge in this scenario. But there's a catch to this reward. This reward expires every 2 weeks. So once a student does perform well and earn a reward because he/she was positively reinforced and now he would like to make sure that he has this badge always with him because it gives him an opportunity to brag about it to his friends, but since the badge will disappear in 2 weeks, it is peer pressure on him after social bragging that he owns the badge. Now the student is supposed to earn more badges to keep in his bucket to make sure he always has one and here is why it is not just the positive reinforcement being applied here, Now the student is performing because of the negative reinforcement. The student is afraid of losing this recognition and it keeps him motivated enough to perform.

Let us look at another example of negative reinforcement with the badge scenario only. Have you noticed LinedIn has introduced a tag for the folks who contribute to their AI based articles?

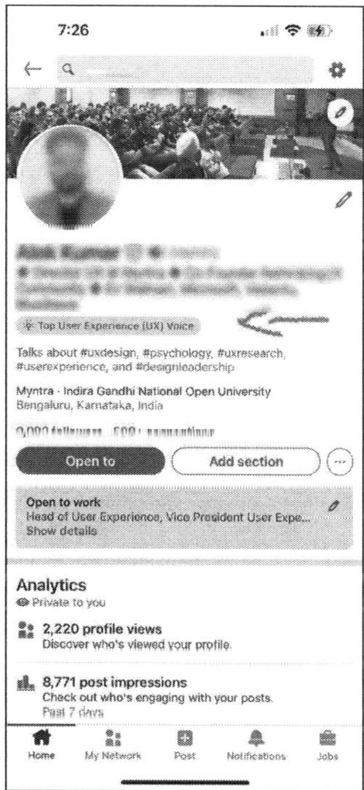

Figure 14.30: LinkedIn badge of top UX Voice

For example, on LinkedIn **Top UX Voice** on any profile, is a tag or badge; this badge is given to a contributor who helps the LinkedIn community with their point of view on different topics. For example, refer to *Figure 14.30*, A gentleman who has been helping folks a lot with UX design point of view, and he got this badge (Top UX Voice) in his profile. Of course, It feels good when someone is rewarded with a particular badge, which is positive reinforcement and this badge actually differentiate this gentleman from the others and make him feel special.

Now, there is a catch with this reward too. This person got this badge because he contributed a lot on LinkedIn, but this badge remains there until he keeps contributing. If he stops contributing consistently, this badge will go away after a certain time. As a contributor, if he wants this badge to be present in his profile, he must contribute consistently. Is it not negative reinforcement now? He must be afraid that he may lose this badge if he stops contributing on LinkedIn. Now he will end up contributing a lot to have this badge attached to his profile.

Hence, in this example positive reinforcement helped to get the badge (Acquisition of a user) and negative reinforcement helped to continue having (Retention of the user) this batch.

Another classy example are games, For example, have a look at *Figure 14.31*, it is for a famous game coin master:

Figure 14.31: Coin master game news

In case you do not know this game's fundamentals, in this game, you earn coins by completing a few activities. But when you are not playing this game, other players may join the game and they may steal your coins. But if you are available at that time or playing the game at the same time, you may save and defend your coins.

It is a classy example of negative reinforcement, where the players keep coming to play the game because if they do not play for a long time, others may steal all their coins. They will not have coins to continue the game.

This negative reinforcement is very common in non-digital spaces as well. The fundamentals of a fine/punishment system are all dependent on negative reinforcement. When people are afraid of paying a huge fine or they are afraid of losing an opportunity or something, they end up following rules. Think of a lot of examples around you. There are a lot of people who follow the rules out of self-awareness and social responsibility as well but there are many folks who follow because they do not want to be punished.

Refer to *Figure 14.32*, When does a referee give a yellow card to a footballer in the game? Of course, when the player makes a mistake and does not follow a particular rule. They are shown a yellow card as a warning. If they ignore and violate the rules, the player may get a red card and the moment they get a red card, they are out of the game.

Figure 14.32: A football player is given a warning yellow card

You will observe negative reinforcement around you on a very large scale. For example: Following traffic rules, because there are rules in place that will make you pay a heavy fine in case you do not follow the rule. And people eventually follow the rules because they do not want to pay a big penalty.

Now you must wonder, which is better? Is negative reinforcement more effective than positive and which one to use and when, right? Let us discuss.

Negative reinforcement is not necessarily less or more effective than positive reinforcement. The effectiveness of each depends on the specific situation, context, and individual in question. Both methods can be potent tools for shifting user behavior, but they operate through different mechanisms. You might first plan to use positive reinforcement in your platform or product and in case it does not work or partially work, you can use negative reinforcement as well.

If you remember my previous example of a student's online classroom and being rewarded with a Speedykid badge, that itself makes it easy to achieve a good amount of engagement and participation from the students but it is possible that students will forget that joyous moment after some time. It has a human tendency to be very aggressive until we achieve something, but the moment we achieve, the value of the achievement goes away in some time. Similarly, students would not have been participating in a similar manner consistently because it is a long-time affair between students and the educator.

But the moment you add a feature that your badge will disappear after two weeks, which is negative reinforcement, now everyone wants to continue participating to make sure that they have at least one badge for sure in their profile. It is possible by just participating consistently. You must notice how positive and negative reinforcement rules are merged to build better engagement here.

Now we will talk about another kind of reinforcement, which is close to positive reinforcement but is provided to the users in a partial manner and step by step. Rewards are never given in one go. Let us understand partial reinforcement.

Partial reinforcement

Partial reinforcement schedules involve providing reinforcement for a behavior inconsistently, not in the same manner each time. This is a contrast with a continuous reinforcement schedule, where reinforcement is given consistently after every behavior. All forms of partial reinforcement lead to behaviors that are more resilient to extinction compared to those formed under continuous reinforcement.

As per the rules of positive reinforcement, we should give some positive reward for completing a task that motivates the user to complete that particular task and if you think it is not working enough, you may add another layer of negative reinforcement to make sure that user is continuously participating. Another route to achieving consistency in participation is through partial reinforcement. It means you give the reward to the user, but in steps, or you give the reward but also convey the benefit of consistently participating or it may be a grand reward after collecting the smaller rewards.

Referring to *Figure 14.33*, this is a very normal scenario with most mobile games. This is the daily missions screen of the game called Teen Patti Gold, which is a card game. In this game, users are supposed to achieve small milestones to achieve some smaller rewards, which is positive reinforcement. Players do compete with other players and win the games while also trying their level best to complete milestone tasks to achieve the rewards. Additionally, there is one big goal that all the players are chasing. In the above screen, you may notice that if players achieve all the smaller milestones, they stand a chance to win a big chest, which may contain up to 500 crore chips (game currency):

Figure 14.33: *A Mobile game daily mission - partial reinforcement*

Another example comes from a game named Coin Master, (which we have previously discussed). Specifically, I would like you to focus on their daily bonus screen, as shown in *Figure 14.34*. In this system, players are encouraged to log in daily to collect a reward, with the promise of a larger reward on the 7th day. This strategy effectively increases player engagement and boosts the number of **daily active users (DAU)** on the platform. The anticipation of the grand reward incentivizes players to log in and collect daily rewards. If there were no milestone rewards, engagement would likely decrease. Without these smaller, incremental rewards, players might feel overwhelmed or demotivated, perceiving the grand reward as too challenging or unattainable. Thus, the use of partial reinforcement serves as an effective gamification technique, striking a balance between motivation and effort (refer to the following figure):

Figure 14.34: Daily bonus in Coin Master

Key takeaways

Reinforcement in design, particularly in the context of user experience (UX) and interaction design, plays a crucial role in shaping user behavior and engagement. The key takeaways from using reinforcement in design include:

- **Behavior shaping:** Reinforcement can be used to encourage desirable user behaviors. Positive reinforcement (like rewards or positive feedback) can increase the likelihood of a behavior being repeated, while negative reinforcement (removing an undesirable element when the desired action is performed) can also be effective.

- **Increased user engagement:** By providing rewards or incentives, designers can boost user engagement. This is evident in gamification strategies where users receive points, badges, or other rewards for completing tasks or reaching milestones.

- **Enhanced user experience:** Reinforcement can improve the overall user experience by making interactions more satisfying and enjoyable. For example, providing immediate feedback on user actions helps in creating a sense of accomplishment and progress.

- **Habit formation:** Consistent and strategically timed reinforcement can lead to habit formation. Users are more likely to return to a product or service if they associate it with positive reinforcement.

- **Motivation and satisfaction:** Reinforcement strategies can increase motivation and satisfaction by rewarding users for their actions. This is especially important in learning environments or task-oriented applications.

In summary, reinforcement in design is a powerful tool that, when used appropriately, can significantly enhance user interaction, satisfaction, and loyalty.

As we have understood so far, reinforcement is a great tool for UX designers to motivate users, build habits, and increase their engagement and retention if it's implemented carefully. I hope you will be able to use this method now in such a manner that your users do not feel offended and engage for a better cause.

In the next chapter, we are going to discuss another gamification element that we experience a lot if we are active on social media. Another element is **shared commitment**. Everyone follows social media a lot and gets easily influenced. Also, when they see their known personalities taking some action on social media, that changes our decision making as well. We will do a deep dive into our own behavior and understand why we behave in a certain manner and how it's used to achieve engagement.

Shared commitment

As suggested by the term **shared commitment**, it refers to a sense of dedication that you and your friends or acquaintances jointly hold. When you both are pursuing the same objective, committing to it and achieving it becomes simpler. Moreover, your trust intensifies significantly when you realize that a person you know well is also taking a similar action

If you observe an acquaintance or friend engaging in a certain behavior, you are more likely to be drawn to that behavior and trust it.

History and origin of shared commitment

The concept of shared commitment in design does not originate from a single theorist or a specific moment in history. Instead, it is a principle that has evolved organically over time, influenced by various theories and practices in design, organizational psychology, and teamwork.

Several movements and methodologies have contributed to this concept:

- **Collaborative design movements:** Historical design movements, such as the Bauhaus and Scandinavian design, emphasized the importance of collaboration and shared goals among designers, architects, and artists.

- **User-Centered Design (UCD):** This approach, which became prominent in the 1980s and 1990s, involves users in the design process. It fostered a shared commitment among designers and users to create effective, user-friendly products.

- **Agile and lean methodologies:** These methodologies, widely adopted in software and product development, emphasize collaboration, flexibility, and continuous improvement. They encourage a shared commitment among team members to achieve common goals.

- **Organizational psychology:** Concepts in organizational psychology about teamwork, group dynamics, and leadership have significantly influenced how shared commitment is understood and applied in design teams.

- **Modern design thinking:** This approach, popularized by organizations like IDEO, stresses empathy, collaboration, and iterative testing. It fosters a shared commitment among diverse team members to solve complex problems.

Therefore, rather than being attributed to a single individual, the concept of shared commitment in design is the result of the convergence of these various influences over time, shaped by the evolving nature of work, technology, and design methodologies.

Shared commitment introduces competition within your known circles and excites you to participate and complete a task or achieve a goal.

Shared commitment is another theory of psychology and persuasive design that is also widely used in game design and UX design. Shared commitment plays a crucial role in joint liability agreements where multiple individuals unite to bear responsibility collectively for a certain goal or outcome. This principle is based on the understanding that every participant is equally invested in the venture's success or failure, creating equal accountabilities for all. It extends beyond individual responsibility, fostering a collective sense of ownership and involvement, which is crucial for the successful realization of the intended results.

To understand it better, let us discuss an example from a mobile game. Referring to *Figure 14.35*, it is the leaderboard of the game where players can see their ranking compared to other players. The top three are getting more visibility, and that excites the players to contribute more and achieve these positions. And I want you to focus on *Figure 14.36*; it is the same leaderboard, but I am checking out the second tab, which is friends. Do you see the difference? This is the leaderboard where I can see the progress and level of my friends (of course, the game has picked up on my social media).

Since the games ask you to sync your social media account or login with social media, on Facebook; they have access to your friends and their level in the same game. But do you notice how this makes a difference? Now that players can see known individuals or their friends on the leaderboard, it is highly likely that players will want to compete and achieve a particular position or may beat their friend in the game to stick to a higher position. It is a classic example of shared commitment; both players are committed to playing the game to beat each other and reach a particular position. With the help of this element, the player ends up being more engaged in the game.

Figure 14.35: A Mobile game leaderboard of players (contd.)

Figure 14.36: A Mobile game leaderboard of players, particularly My Friends

Referring to *Figure 14.37*, it is a social media post on one of the most famous platforms, which is Instagram. If you notice it carefully, it is a sponsored post by a brand/Instagram handle called **nasher_miles**, and the user does not follow this. The user is shown this advertisement/post with a very strong shared commitment that one of your friends follows this account. It says followed by **poonamdebghosh** and 30.5K others. It adds some credibility to this Instagram account, and as a user, I am more likely to check it out or may end up following it too. These are the tricks being used by social media platforms a lot to gain more followers and click-through rates on their ads and posts. You could use this element of persuasive design to engage with your users and get better attention:

Figure 14.37: *One of the posts of Instagram*

Let us look at another non-gaming example from another social media site that is famous for professional networking. Yes, you are correct; it is LinkedIn.

Refer to *Figure 14.38*, the screen when you complete a particular course on the LinkedIn learning platform. You can share the details of the course you completed with the link to the course. By sharing this on social media, a user encourages their friends and social media followers to observe this and know about the achievements of friends and acquaintances. It motivates others to get influenced and complete the course for themselves as well. A shared commitment here is to motivate others to complete a particular task. On various platforms, sometimes users may post when they start or post their progress and they may invite others to join them and then all of them jointly achieve the task.

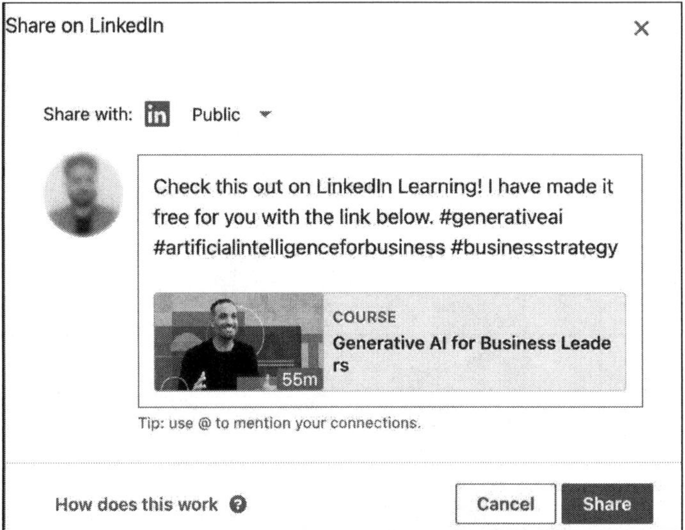

Figure 14.38: LinkedIn shares a course when completed

Overall, shared commitment is a great element of design and psychology to follow and apply to gain more attention from the users, get more participation, and help in completing a particular task by getting influenced by others or by a joint activity or teamwork.

In summary, we learned about shared commitment as an element of psychology, persuasive design, and gamification. We discussed how Few games and other platforms, like social media, are utilizing this theory to engage their users, build the nature of competition, and encourage teamwork to achieve a particular task. You may use these tips and tricks to apply in our day-to-day product design when you want to engage the user but for that, you will have to take advantage of the user's social media data. Do not forget to be conscious, because respecting privacy is the most critical element in building trust among your users. As a platform, if you do not have access to user's social media information, it is highly likely that you won't be able to apply the element of sharing commitment. So, take the consensus and then encourage and influence the users.

Conclusion

With this chapter, we are done with the gamification part of the chapters in the book. But that is not all. There are a lot more gamification elements and elements of persuasive design, like framing, salience, breakage, and a few more. I highly encourage you to read about all those. I tried to cover the most important ones.

In the next chapters, we will discuss the biases that we, as humans, have. As human we all have some biases because of the way we have grown up, the kind of culture we have lived in, etc. We will discuss biases and their types in the coming chapters, and we will start with confirmation biases. Confirmation bias particularly talks about how humans try to figure out the evidence to prove what they know or think.

Section IV
Biases

Design, like many fields, is subject to various cognitive biases that can affect how designers create and users perceive and interact with products. Understanding these biases is crucial for creating more effective and user-centered designs. Here are some common biases in design:

CHAPTER 15

Biases in UX Design

Introduction

Bias is essentially an inclination towards a particular viewpoint, often at the expense of a neutral stance. This tendency is influenced by an individual's personal beliefs, experiences, or preferences, impacting their thoughts, actions, and choices, both knowingly and unknowingly. Various types of biases exist, including cultural, gender, racial, and confirmation biases.

Broadly speaking, the concept of bias is crucial in discussions about fairness and neutrality, especially in sectors like journalism, science, and law, where objectivity is key. Acknowledging and addressing biases in these areas is vital to ensuring that outcomes, decisions, or reports are not improperly swayed by personal or systemic leanings.

From a psychological standpoint, biases are acknowledged as part of the brain's cognitive mechanisms. They act as mental shortcuts or heuristics to streamline the processing of information, yet they can also result in flawed judgments or decision-making.

In the context of modern technology and extensive data, bias is increasingly relevant to **Artificial Intelligence (AI)** and **Machine Learning (ML)**. In these fields, biases present in algorithms or data can produce distorted or unjust results, thereby mirroring and potentially exacerbating prevailing social biases.

Structure

The chapter will cover the following topics:

- Confirmation bias
- Negativity bias
- Research bias
- Default bias
- Anchoring bias

Objectives

Bias in design refers to the systematic and often unintentional preferences or inclinations that influence the design process, leading to skewed outcomes. To mitigate bias in design, it is important to adopt inclusive design practices, actively seek diverse perspectives, use comprehensive and representative data, and continuously test and iterate designs with a wide range of users.

In this chapter we will discuss about few Biases that impacts are design. It is very important to be aware of those biases and take adequate action when required. We will discuss about confirmation bias, negativity bias, research bias, default bias and anchoring bias. We will also look at the real use cases of these biases through product design and learn from those biases.

So let us start with the first one.

Confirmation bias

People want to confirm what they think is correct.

Confirmation bias occurs when individuals seek out, interpret, favor, and remember information in a manner that validates or reinforces their pre-existing beliefs or values. This bias is evident when people focus on information that aligns with their views while disregarding opposing data, or when they interpret vague evidence as corroborative of their existing positions. The bias is especially evident in outcomes that are desired. on topics that are emotionally significant, and for beliefs that are firmly established. While overcoming confirmation bias is a challenging task for many, it can be mitigated through methods such as education and the development of critical thinking abilities.

History

An early example of confirmation bias was demonstrated in *Peter Watson's* 1960 experiment, where participants were tasked with discerning the experimenter's numerical sequencing rule. The study revealed that subjects tended to select responses that aligned with their own hypotheses, disregarding evidence to the contrary. This occurred even when their hypotheses were incorrect, leading them to quickly develop confidence in these erroneous beliefs (Gray, 2010, p. 356). The phenomenon of confirmation bias, although observed in psychological research over time, was formally named in a 1977 paper that conducted an experimental study on this subject (Mynatt, Doherty, and Tweney, 1977).

Confirmation bias in psychology refers to the inclination to prioritize information that aligns with one's pre-existing beliefs or values. Individuals who display this bias tend to actively seek, interpret, recall, and place greater emphasis on information that validates their perspectives. Simultaneously, they often overlook, disregard, or minimize the importance of data that are challenges or that contradict their existing viewpoints.

Let us understand confirmation bias via the diagram below (refer to *Figure 15.1*). There are always facts and evidence for any topic and discussion; moreover, because of our culture, way of life, and the way we grow up, we have some beliefs. There is always common ground between what we believe and facts. That overlap area contains the facts and evidence that we have because of our bias and that is called confirmation bias. Please refer to the following figure:

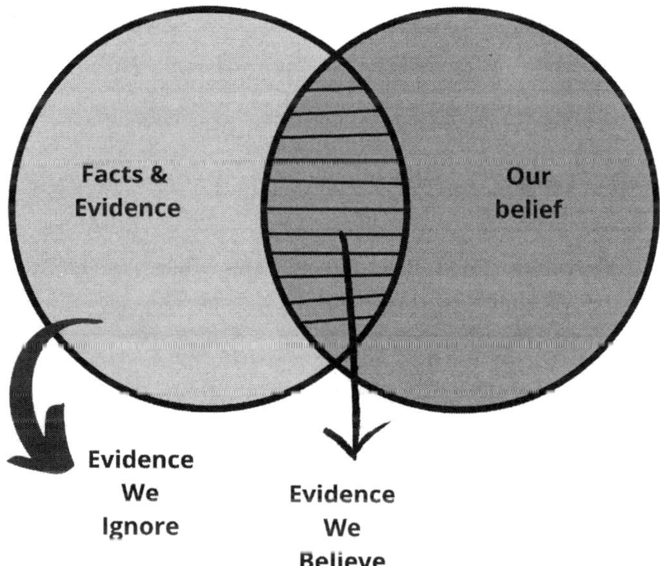

Figure 15.1: *Confirmation bias*

Now, the let us discuss, here are 2 questions (Asked to a user in an interview regarding a design):

1. Do you think this red button is helpful to proceed further? vs.
2. What would you do to proceed further?

The first question has some bias from the person who is asking the question. It has some leading answer hidden in it. Looks like it is already believed that this red button is helpful but just trying to get confirmation from the users.

Here are common examples of how confirmation bias often appears:

*   Individuals often neglect information that contradicts their pre-existing beliefs, largely due to the influence of ego, which can impede impartial thinking.
*   The discomfort caused by conflicting information leads to a preference for data that affirms their beliefs.
*   This confirmation bias not only provides a sense of ease in processing information but also reinforces their convictions, bolstering self-assurance in those beliefs.
*   These bias manifests when individuals selectively collect or remember information, or when they interpret it from a skewed perspective.
*   It can be observed in situations such as listening to only one side of a news story or understanding the story in a way that aligns with their existing beliefs.

The impact of confirmation bias is more pronounced in matters that are emotionally charged or pertain to deeply held beliefs, such as issues related to religion, race, politics, women's rights, or climate change.

In the context of UX, the level of investment in one's design assumptions or user perceptions significantly influences the strength of confirmation bias. For instance, if a designer has devoted several months to developing a design, they are more inclined to favor usability feedback that affirms their design and be skeptical of any evidence indicating design flaws. Conversely, if the designer spent only a day or two on a paper prototype before conducting a usability study, they are likely to be less biased when interpreting the study's outcomes.

To mitigate the effects of confirmation bias in UX design, it is essential for designers and researchers to proactively explore diverse perspectives and incorporate a wide array of opinions in their decision-making process. This involves soliciting input from an array of stakeholders, conducting user research with participants from different backgrounds, and continuously seeking alternative viewpoints throughout the design journey.

Tips to prevent confirmation bias

Acknowledging the presence of confirmation bias is the initial step in circumventing it. For UX researchers and designers, here are several strategies to prevent falling prey to confirmation bias:

- **Early access to the data**: As discussed earlier, designers get biased when they work on designs for a long time and remain less biased when they have done just the low fidelity wireframes. So, the lower your investment in terms of time, resources, and emotional attachment to a particular design, the more objective you will likely be when evaluating feedback from user research. Therefore, obtaining empirical data from your target audience at an early stage increases the likelihood of analyzing and responding to the findings with minimal bias.

- **Focus on discovery research rather than validation**: UX experts must approach their work with a mindset geared towards exploring and examining hypotheses and assumptions, rather than merely seeking to confirm them. The primary aim of research should be to discover new insights, rather than merely affirm preconceived notions. Designers need to be adaptable, promptly acknowledging when a design direction is proving unfruitful, instead of investing further time and resources into a potentially ineffective solution. It is crucial to ensure that the planning phase of any user study encompasses a thorough evaluation of the study's objectives.

- **No leading or bias questions**: When UX professionals collect user feedback, be it through usability tests, diary studies, or interviews, it is important to steer clear of suggestive questions. Such questions can inadvertently guide participants towards specific issues or responses that researchers might be focused on, thereby influencing the authenticity of their reactions. Leading and bias questions will give biased responses and UX professionals end up getting responses that may mislead your output and design decision depending on the output.

- **Stay neutral during user research**: As an expert UX professional, you are supposed to be neutral during usability testing and user interviews. When I say neutral, it means you are not supposed to show the expression of being surprised, happy, frustrated, sad, etc. These expressions give some clues to the respondents during the usability testing, and they might start behaving in a way that makes you happy. You will show your emotions because of your confirmation biases, and that is something that you are supposed to ignore.

- **Employ multiple sources of data collection**: By integrating various data sources, you not only enhance the reliability of your research but also mitigate the risk of confirmation biases. While it may be tempting to interpret a single research outcome to fit a hypothesis, aligning data from diverse origins like user testing, analytics, quantitative studies, or customer service records presents a more challenging scenario for such bias.

- **Incorporate new perspectives into your research planning and analysis**: Where feasible, seek the input of a colleague who is not closely connected with your project to review your study plan and participate in the presentation of results. A person with no preconceived notions or knowledge about previous assumptions can offer a fresh, unbiased viewpoint, aiding in the identification and mitigation of confirmation bias more effectively.

Confirmation bias can lead individuals to rigidly adhere to erroneous beliefs or to disproportionately emphasize information that aligns with their pre-existing notions. In the realm of UX, this bias can obscure objective judgment, hinder empathy with users, result in poorly structured research, and lead to the misinterpretation of feedback. Recognizing the influence of confirmation bias on both the researchers' interpretations and users' reactions is crucial for UX professionals. By employing effective methods for gathering unbiased, actionable data, UX practitioners can create products that are more effectively designed and user centric.

I hope you have a good understanding of confirmation bias now and will be able to recognize your own confirmation bias, or at least be aware that you can do justice to your research and design.

In the next chapters, we will discuss the next bias, which is negativity bias. That is very normal and frequently and easily observable by the normal user. We do recall and remember our negative experiences more than our positive ones. We will discuss this and also discuss how it impacts design decisions and what should be done by designers to not become the victims of this bias.

Negativity bias

Negative experience stays in your memory for longer period.

Negativity bias is a psychological tendency where negative events exert a stronger impact on our mental state compared to positive events of equivalent intensity. This means that we experience negative occurrences with greater intensity, even when they are of the same magnitude as positive ones. Due to this bias, we end up building the mindset that the concern is way bigger than what exactly it is. Negativity stays in our memory for so long, and so do your users who use your app/website, or digital product. Once the user has a negative experience, it is going to be difficult to convert them to a positive note.

History

The concept of negativity bias has its roots in evolutionary psychology and has been a subject of interest in psychological research for many decades. The history and development of this concept involve several key stages:

- **Evolutionary basis**: The idea of negativity bias is often linked to evolutionary psychology. The theory suggests that paying more attention to negative threats in the environment was crucial for the survival of early humans. Being attuned to potential dangers (like predators or natural hazards) was more immediately consequential than noticing positive stimuli.

- **Early psychological research**: In the 20th century, psychological research began to explore how people process negative and positive information differently. Pioneering studies in the 1960s and 1970s started to document that individuals tend to give greater weight to negative experiences or emotions compared to positive ones.

- **The 1980s and 1990s**: During this period, negativity bias became a more defined concept within psychology. Researchers like *Paul Rozin* and *Edward Royzman* further explored the idea, noting that negative experiences have a greater impact on an individual's psychological state than positive experiences of the same intensity.

- **Recent applications**: In contemporary psychology, the concept of negativity bias has been applied to understand various aspects of human behavior and mental health, such as anxiety disorders, depression, relationship dynamics, and decision-making processes.

Negativity bias is now a well-established concept in psychology and neuroscience, highlighting the fundamental ways in which negative experiences influence human cognition, emotion, and behavior.

This is our inclination to not only notice negative experiences more easily but also to focus on them longer. Also referred to as positive-negative asymmetry, this bias causes us to experience the discomfort of criticism more intensely than the pleasure of commendation.

This bias sheds light on why it is hard to change a bad first impression and why past traumas can have enduring effects. In most situations, we are more likely to pick up on and later vividly recall negative aspects.

As humans, we typically:

- Remember negative experiences more clearly than positive ones.
- Retain memories of insults more than compliments.
- Have a stronger reaction to negative events.
- Frequently, dwell on negative thoughts over positive ones.
- Show a more intense response to negative occurrences compared to positive ones of the same magnitude.

For instance, imagine you are having a good day at work, but a colleague says something that annoys you. You might spend the rest of the day fixated on that comment.

Then, when you return home and are asked about your day, you might describe it as terrible, even though it was generally positive, except for that one negative experience.

Negativity bias in UX design

A single usability issue on your website will have a greater impact than the multitude of positive attributes it possesses.

In usability studies, participants often remain silent when the **user interface** (**UI**) meets their expectations. A seamless experience, despite the significant effort put in by the UX team and developers, typically goes uncommented and unnoticed. However, when the interaction falls short of their expectations, users tend to become critical and retain a lasting memory of the issue. You may realize that users tend to write negative feedback for your product at any feedback session, at Play Store/App Store review or in the reviews section. But if they have a seamless experience, they are not bothered to write about their awesome experience.

If mere usability is the standard, then websites and applications need to be extraordinary to stand out and be memorable. So, how do you satisfy discerning users who are quick to react negatively to even the smallest errors? Here are some strategies to consider:

Negativity bias should not impact your design

Unique interactions and design patterns demand additional effort due to their unfamiliarity, as users might be experiencing the patterns very first time. It has some amount of learning curve. When looking for navigation or search functions on a website, users typically anticipate finding them in the usual locations that are common across many other sites, (similar to Jakob's law in *Chapter 4, Jakob's Law*)

You must consider that users tend to look for the search option at the top, **Sign Up** at the top right, **Hamburger** (menu icons in mobile) icon at top left, company logo at top left, etc. If you are going to change these patterns, you might look different for sure, but it will make it difficult for users to find them. For example, in *Figure 15.2*, you will notice the **Staples** homepage had their logo in the center previously but they moved their logo to the left in the recent homepage, due to socially strategic reasons and user behavior patterns:

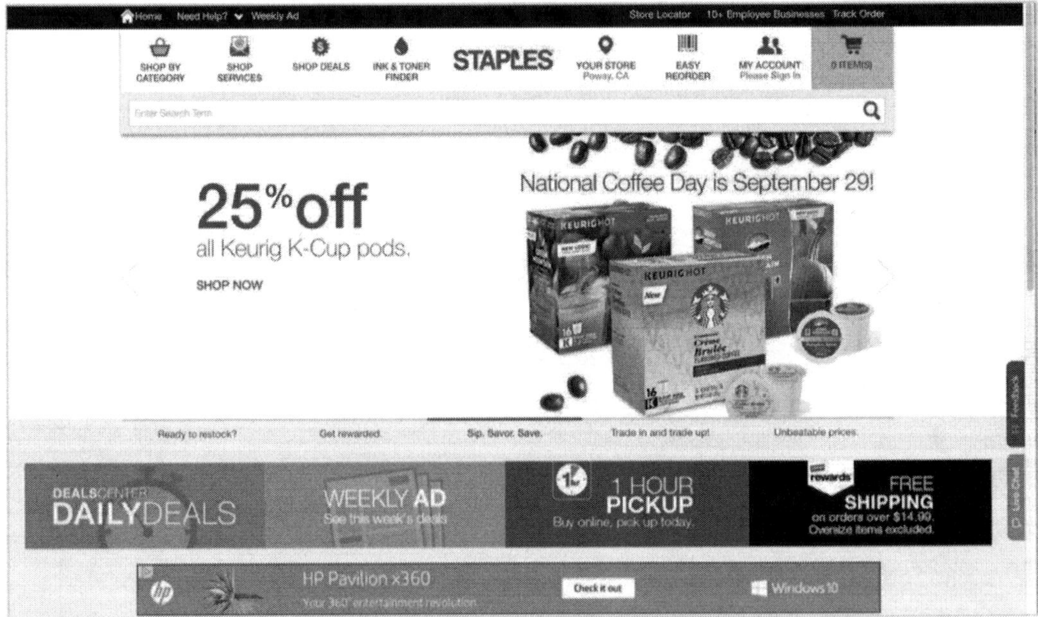

Figure 15.2: Staples previous homepage

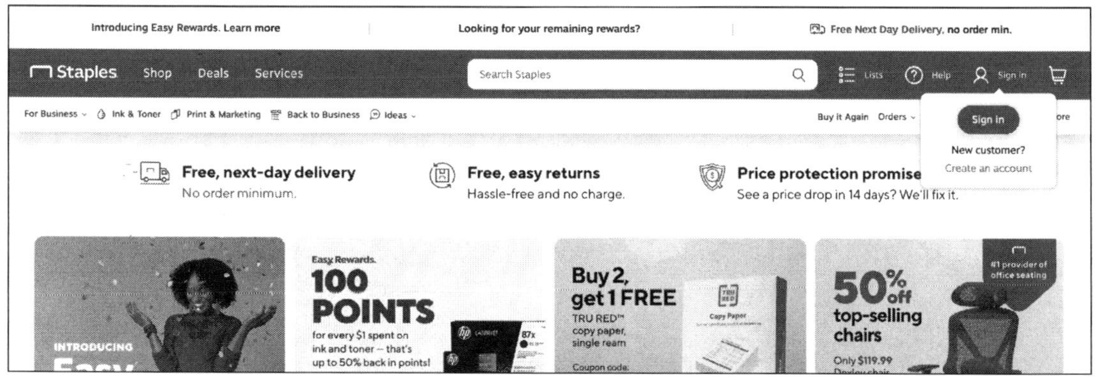

Figure 15.3: Staples current homepage

- **Match user flow and expectations**: Users carry preconceived notions about how a system should function and the steps required to complete tasks. When workflows are cumbersome, displaying information inappropriately or in an unexpected sequence, disrupts the users' sense of control, leading to frustration.

  A frequent error among UX designers is valuing efficiency over user expectations. Occasionally, more extended user journeys are preferable if they align with what users anticipate. On the other hand, shorter, albeit non-standard, user flows might cause users to pause and reflect, which is not always ideal.

- **Prepare for and mitigate users' worries**: Positive experiences can be shaped in many ways, with microcopy playing a crucial role. These brief snippets of text offer guidance or soothe concerns, greatly enhancing positive perceptions and preventing negative impressions before they arise. Microcopy is particularly effective when it is delivered at the right moment, within the appropriate context, is clear and straightforward, and carries a suitable tone of voice.

- **Use relevant images and gratification in your content**: As I have discussed in previous chapters, images have better recall than just text. And it's easy for users to remember. So try to use images to make the screens interesting and easy to consume. For example, refer to *Figures 15.4* and *15.5*, These are screenshots of the categories screen of Myntra (online shopping app), They could have easily kept only the names of categories to browse the desired category page, but they used relevant images to make it more prominent, easy to scan, and recall. It also adds a flavor of rich design and creative innovation.

Please refer to the following figure:

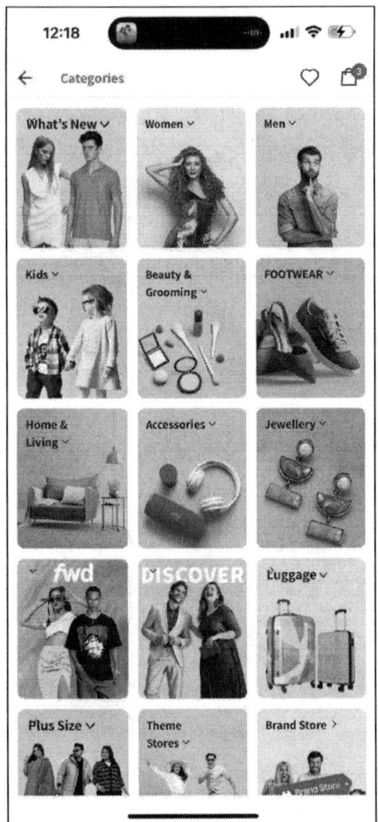

Figure 15.4: Myntra category screen

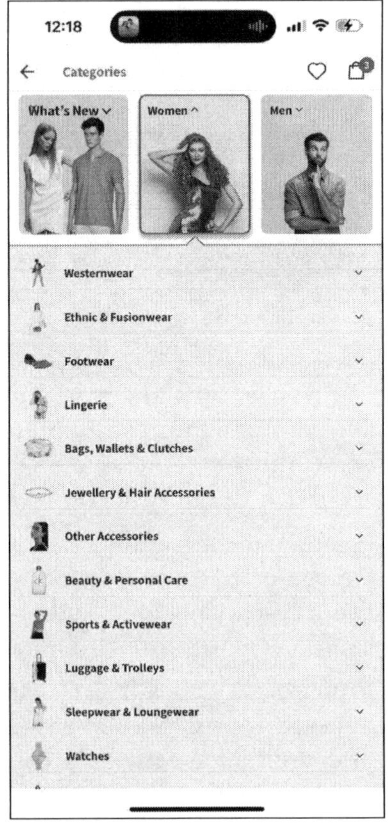

Figure 15.5: Myntra sub-category screen

- **Write user friendly error message**: Even with diligent efforts to ensure a seamless user experience, websites occasionally require error messages to assist users in addressing inevitable issues.

  While encountering error messages is generally unwelcome, they can act as substitutes for customer service support when needed. Abrasive or unclear messages can transform minor issues into hostile experiences. Conversely, polite, and informative messages have the potential to defuse situations that could otherwise escalate into significant problems.

- **Introduce gratification micro interactions**: Users are very impatient, and you need to engage them in case you want them to wait for you / your product to respond. Use some micro interaction to keep them informed or engaged so that they are not clueless, because being clueless will bring anxiety and negativity bias immediately.

- **Usability test**: Most importantly, do not forget to test your designs with real users. It is said - some research is better than no research and it is highly advisable to show your designs to few users, even if you conduct gorilla testing, but you must test your flow or design before it goes live.

Some research is better than no research, so test your design, before you go live.

It is highly likely that users will highlight a small mistake and will never notice your flawless screens and flow because they are not looking at your screens, they are just experiencing it. When the experience is awesome, users do not tend to notice, just feel better. That is the reality of negativity bias. Users themselves have no idea why they react in a certain manner because negativity bias drives their actions.

So as designers, we must make sure that the first impression is awesome and make sure we follow UX rules and processes to make the screen flawless and beautiful.

I hope you have a good understanding of negativity bias now and will be able to recognize your user's negativity bias drivers. It is fruitful if you are aware of these biases before they reach the users and fix them.

In the next section, we will discuss the next bias, which is research bias. That is very important, especially for the researchers and designers who conduct user research.

We will discuss how your bias impacts your research outcome.

Research bias

Human's own biases impact research outcomes.

To put it simply, research bias occurs when the researcher, whether intentionally or not, influences the methodology of a study, thereby affecting its outcomes. In essence, research bias is the distortion of research results due to the way the researcher conducts the investigation.

Research bias does not necessarily stem from deliberate actions. It often arises from a study that is not well-designed, or from difficulties in obtaining a diverse and appropriate sample. While the goal is to achieve complete objectivity, it is usually inevitable to encounter some degree of bias in any research undertaking.

History

The history of research bias is closely linked to the development of survey research and statistics over the years. Let us explore some key milestones:

- **Early days of surveying (before 20th century)**: While the concept of surveying dates to ancient civilizations, the formal understanding of bias in surveys was not a significant focus. Early surveys, such as censuses and demographic studies, were more concerned with data collection than with the nuances of bias.

- **Emergence of modern statistics (early 20th century)**: The formal study of statistics began to take shape in the early 20th century. Pioneers like *Karl Pearson* and *Ronald Fisher* contributed to statistical theory, but the focus was still more on the development of statistical methods than on survey bias specifically.

- **Social research expansion (1950s and 1960s)**: As social sciences grew, so did the reliance on surveys. This period saw an increasing focus on minimizing bias, leading to developments in survey design, question wording, and interview techniques.

- **Technological advancements (late 20th century)**: The advent of computers and later the internet brought significant changes. While these technologies made surveys easier to conduct and analyze, they also introduced new biases, like those related to online survey participation.

- **Contemporary challenges and solutions**: Today, survey bias is a well-recognized issue, with ongoing research into how to identify and reduce it. Challenges like non-response bias, response bias, and others are the focus of much current research. The rise of big data and alternative data collection methods also presents new opportunities and challenges for addressing survey bias.

The history of research bias is a testament to the evolving nature of research methods and the continuous effort to achieve more accurate and reliable results in social science, market research, public opinion polling, and other fields reliant on survey data.

Research bias significantly impacts the integrity of the research process, leading to potentially misleading or incorrect outcomes. Here are some ways this bias might influence the research process:

- **Compromised research design**: Bias in research can lead to skewed or inaccurate results, undermining the reliability and validity of the study. If bias influences the setup of the study, the data collection methods, or the analysis approach, it can introduce systematic errors that may impact the outcome of your research badly.

- **Questionable conclusions**: Bias in research can cast doubts on the validity of a study's findings. Biased methodologies can result in unsupported or erroneous claims, as the outcomes may not accurately represent reality or comprehensively address the research question.

- **Incorrect interpretations**: Bias can lead to erroneous interpretations of research findings, affecting the overall understanding of the research issue. Researchers might be inclined to interpret results in a way that aligns with their preconceptions or expectations, neglecting alternative explanations or conflicting evidence.

- **Ethical implications**: Research bias raises ethical issues. It can adversely impact individuals, groups, or society at large. Biased research can lead to misinformation in its decision-making processes, culminating in ineffective policies, interventions, or treatments.

- **Erosion of trust**: Bias in research erodes the credibility of science. Biased studies can diminish public trust in scientific research and lower confidence in using scientific evidence for decision-making purposes.

Types of research bias

There are multiple research biases, and we will discuss the some of the most important ones here:

- **Selection bias / sampling bias**: This occurs when an unrepresentative sample distorts the outcomes.

- **Analysis bias**: This arises when the chosen method or approach of analysis results in biased findings.

- **Procedural bias**: This happens when the way a study is conducted, particularly in terms of data collection, influences who participates and how they respond.

Let us discuss them in detail

Selection / sampling bias

Selection bias arises when the design of a study inherently excludes a pertinent group from the research, adversely affecting the results' quality.

With selection bias, the outcomes of the study are inclined towards the group it includes or favors, leading to potentially biased conclusions. For instance, a study on government policies that only involves participants who support a specific political party will yield biased outcomes, as it omits the perspectives of supporters of other parties.

Selection bias is particularly prevalent in quantitative research because the chosen sampling method can significantly influence the statistical outcomes. However, it is also a concern in qualitative research due to the possibility of unbalanced samples. Therefore, it is crucial to carefully consider the composition of your sample and select a sampling strategy that is consistent with your research objectives. While achieving a perfect sample is rare, it is important to recognize potential biases in your sample and take them into account when analyzing the data

For example, if you are conducting research on the payment flow of an app, you may have framed some questions for the survey and sent it to a specific set of audience. Now, if you want to run a survey about your payment flow, you should take feedback from - frequent buyers of the app, occasional buyers of your app or users who initiated the payment but dropped in between. But what if you sent the survey to the users who never bought anything or who never initiated a payment. Do you think you will get the correct response? No. This is a sample or selection bias. and it is very important for all of us to choose the right sample for our quantitative and qualitative research. In short, it is important to **ask the right question to the right audience to get the right response**. None of the above can be compromised.

Analysis bias

Analysis bias takes place when the analysis process either emphasizes or downplays specific data points to support a particular outcome, often aligning with the researcher's anticipated result or hypothesis. This means that analysis bias occurs when there is preferential presentation of data that backs a specific idea or hypothesis, rather than impartially showcasing all data.

For instance, in a study examining consumer opinions about a particular product, you might focus more on analyzing data that shows positive feedback about the product, while giving less attention to data reflecting negative views. Essentially, you would be selectively highlighting data that aligns with your preferred findings, thereby introducing bias in the information presented by the study.

This type of bias is not exclusive to quantitative research; it can also manifest in qualitative studies. Such bias might not always be deliberate or even recognized by the researcher, especially given the inherent subjectivity in qualitative research. Humans naturally tend to seek out and interpret information in ways that affirm their pre-existing beliefs or values, a phenomenon known as confirmation bias in psychology. Therefore, it is crucial not to assume that analysis bias is always a conscious choice and to be vigilant against it, as it can subtly influence any researcher's work.

Procedural bias

Procedural bias, also known as administration bias, is a subtle but significant form of bias that can arise during the administration of a study, particularly in the data collection phase. It is crucial to recognize and mitigate this bias. This bias occurs when the participant of the research is influenced by anyone or anything.

An example of procedural bias is when study participants face constraints while providing information. For instance, if participants are rushed to complete a survey, such as during a brief lunch break, they may submit incomplete or hastily filled responses that does not accurately represent their true opinions.

Procedural bias can also occur through inappropriate incentives for participation. Offering rewards for survey completion might lead participants to give false or hurried responses just to claim the reward. This could also attract a specific type of respondent, such as those seeking freebies, thereby skewing the sample away from the intended demographic.

The format of data collection can contribute to procedural bias too. Conducting surveys or interviews exclusively online might inadvertently exclude individuals who lack technological proficiency, appropriate devices, or reliable internet access. Conversely, some might find in-person interviews intimidating or the physical setting uncomfortable, such as being observed by others during the interview. These factors can all lead to less reliable data, underscoring the need to carefully consider the data collection method to minimize procedural bias.

While there are numerous other types of research bias, we can only address a few in this context. Therefore, it is important to acquaint yourself with as many potential biases as possible to reduce the likelihood of research bias affecting your study.

User research is such an important element of design, and as a designer and researcher, it is your duty to make sure that you do not get biased and that your results are not impacted because of your bias, your cultural beliefs, and your own thought process. We discussed the types of research bias during qualitative and quantitative research.

I hope you have a good understanding of research bias now and will be able to recognize your own bias towards the research you are conducting. It is very important to be aware of research bias and act before it is too late, because ignoring biases in research may skew the complete output of your research.

In the next chapters, we will discuss the next bias, which is the **default bias**. We will discuss how conventional methods overpower your decisions and users tend to stick to established behaviors.

Default bias

Users do not like change.

In the absence of a strong motivation to switch, individuals often remain with the default choice, be it a suggestion, option, or product. Decision-making typically demands effort, and it is simpler for people to go along with the default choice.

No one likes change without knowing if this change is good or bad for them. People are usually comfortable with what they have and there are many instances where people do not even want to explore other options. They get so comfortable with the current and default options with them that they do not want to bother to explore other options. This is a bias that most of us have and it is called default bias.

History

The concept of default bias, also known as **default effect** or **status quo bias**, has its roots in behavioral economics and psychology. It is a part of a larger set of cognitive biases that affect human decision-making and behavior. Here is a brief overview of its history and development:

- **Behavioral economics foundations**: The field of behavioral economics, which blends elements of psychology and economics, has been crucial in understanding default bias. Traditional economics assumes rational decision-making, but behavioral economics recognizes that humans often act irrationally due to various biases and cognitive limitations.

- **Tversky and Kahneman's work**: The groundwork for understanding default bias was laid by psychologists *Amos Tversky* and *Daniel Kahneman* in the 1970s. Their work on prospect theory and heuristics and biases, such as loss aversion and the endowment effect, provided insights into why people might prefer the status quo.

- **Recognition of status quo bias**: The specific term *status quo bias* was popularized in a 1988 paper by *William Samuelson* and *Richard Zeckhauser*. They noticed that people tend to stick to their current situation (the status quo) even when a change would be beneficial. This bias was observed in various scenarios, including consumer choices, investment decisions, and policy preferences.

- **Recent trends and digital context**: With the rise of digital technology and online platforms, default bias has gained attention in the context of user interface design, digital marketing, and online consumer behavior.

The history of default bias is a testament to the evolving understanding of human psychology in economic and decision-making contexts, demonstrating that our choices are often less about rational deliberation and more influenced by the context and presentation of options.

Inertia acts as a powerful factor in maintaining the status quo for many individuals, regardless of the implications.

Have you ever considered why Google is the default search engine when you use your phone to search for something? Although, switching to Yahoo, Bing, or Amazon is just a simple click away, most people refrain from making the switch. A recent article in *The New York Times* revealed that Google spends heavily to be the preferred choice on web browsers and mobile devices, paying $100 million annually to be the default search engine on Firefox. At first glance, it might not seem worth it to pay so much just to be one click ahead of competitors. Yet, the reality is that despite the ease of switching, very few people do, keeping Google as the default option.

This tendency to stick with the default option is known as default bias (or status quo bias), reflecting our inclination towards inaction and our preference to adhere to choices we have already made. Researchers have identified four key reasons for this bias:

- First, changing from the default involves mental effort or a **cognitive cost**, leading people to conserve their decision-making energy or, to simply put it, to avoid effort.

- Second, inertia is a powerful factor that keeps many people in their current state.

- Third, individuals are more averse to losses than they are attracted to equivalent gains, so they often stick with the default to prevent potential losses that could come from a change in behavior.

- Lastly, there is an underlying assumption that if something is set as the default, it must be a good choice, which encourages more people to accept it without question.

So, generally if you seek your user's attention to click a button and accept or apply a change, the adoption rate is going to be really challenging. For example, if you want your users to enroll to a membership plan, which could be for free of cost while the users get some extra benefit due to that. I have seen in my previous experience that even if the users are getting such a beneficial deal, users are not willing to switch to this new view or subscribe to a new plan. Have you ever faced this? Do you think why they are not willing to opt in for this new program? There are multiple reasons:

- The users are so comfortable with the current setting / offering that he / she do not feel a need to even explore a new plan / offer.

- The users fear losing the current setup. Hence, whatever a user has, whether it is good, bad, best, magnificent, etc. is something that they like.

- Few users are lazy about the learning curve. Everyone is not comfortable spending time in consuming new information and new way of experiencing something. Once they explore, they might like and maybe love the change but it is uncomfortable accepting change in general.

Now the question is how designers should handle these situations where users are not willing to adapt to a new change and they are very strict about their default bias. Moreover, how to use the default bias to help the users.

Default bias in UX design

Here are a few tips to help the designers to use default bias in design:

- **Preferable options by default selected**: There are a lot of merits in keeping few checkboxes by default selected in a form where it is evident and easier for users to access. This will help users save some time as well as the probability of unchecking is a bit lesser.

Note: Please ignore keeping options by default selected in the case of financial stuff or something where you really need user consent in legal matters.

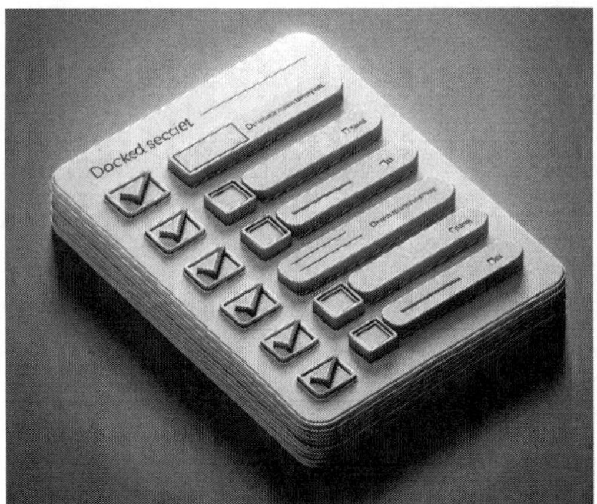

Figure 15.6: A form has few checkboxes by default selected

- **Try opt out**: Let us suppose, there is a beneficial program for the users and you want all your users to be enrolled for the program; one way is that, you ask your users to Opt in for the program where you might struggle with the adoption (number of users enrollment) and Users might be very comfortable with their current setup. Please refer to the following figure:

Figure 15.7: A congratulation screen with option to opt out

You may try another method that you by default give access of your new program to all the users and give them the option to opt out prominently. This could be an impactful decision for getting more enrollment to your product and the users who really do not want to continue, they can opt out and stick to their current setup.

Be very cautious while going for this opt out route because it might backfire as well. Few users might get surprised and uncomfortable with the new setup and they may leave your platform if they have not already spent a good amount of time. They might struggle to figure out how to opt out. Hence, it is extremely important to make opt out (option to unregister from the program) so obvious that users do not struggle. You also should not forget to take the opinion of your legal team because in certain cases, you might need the user's consent before you change their experience.

"Encourage healthier behavior by making it the default, requiring an active choice only to opt out."

Users typically modify their settings based on the provided default values, often using these defaults as a reference point and assuming them to be optimal. This approach to default values improves the overall user experience.

Default bias is a very strong bias and a great comfort zone but it is possible with many tips and trick, you need to figure out ways to encourage your users to adapt to the new and beneficial change.

I hope you have a good understanding of default bias now and will be able to recognize your own and your user's default bias while changing something that was consistently in place. It is very important to be aware of the default bias of the users while designing the layout and offers for them.

In the next section, we will discuss the last bias of my book, which is the **anchoring bias**. We will discuss how anchoring bias makes users rely heavily on the first piece of information they see and how designers utilize this bias and how to make sure that your design is not the victim of this anchoring bias.

Anchoring bias

Users trust that the first information is always correct.

Anchoring bias, also known as adjustment bias, is the inclination to overly rely on one specific piece of information when making decisions. This bias leads us to use an initial value as a reference point, significantly impacting our decisions based on this anchor. Effective anchors can guide users in establishing what is considered normal or exceptional.

In the realm of UX design, the anchoring bias significantly influences how users make decisions and perceive products. Designers need to be cognizant of this bias to craft the best user experiences and steer clear of possible drawbacks.

History

The concept of anchoring bias has its roots in the field of psychology and behavioral economics, and it has been a subject of interest and study for several decades. Here is an overview of its history:

- **Tversky and Kahneman's research**: The term **anchoring bias** was popularized in the 1970s by two psychologists, *Amos Tversky* and *Daniel Kahneman*. They conducted seminal experiments and studies that demonstrated how people make estimates by starting from an initial value (anchor) and adjusting away from it. Their work laid the foundation for understanding how anchoring affects decision-making.

- **1974 experiment**: One of their most famous experiments, conducted in 1974, involved asking participants to estimate the percentage of African countries in the United Nations. Before estimating, participants spun a wheel with numbers on it, which was rigged to stop either at 10 or 65. *Tversky* and *Kahneman* found that those who saw the wheel stop at 10 guessed lower percentages than those who saw it stop at 65, illustrating how an arbitrary number could influence judgments.

- **Inclusion in prospect theory**: *Kahneman* later incorporated anchoring bias into his broader theory of decision-making under uncertainty, known as **prospect theory**, for which he was awarded the Nobel Prize in Economic Sciences in 2002 (*Tversky* had passed away by this time).

- **Current understanding and usage**: Today, anchoring bias is recognized as a common cognitive bias that can lead to errors in judgment and decision-making. It is a concept taught in psychology, economics, marketing, and other fields to help understand and predict human behavior.

The history of anchoring bias illustrates how our understanding of human decision-making has evolved, especially regarding the influence of initial information on our judgments and choices. In this chapter, we will also discuss how anchoring bias influences the decisions of users and how it impacts UX design.

Problems arise when your starting point turns out to be your sticking point.

Apple's CEO *Steve Jobs* delivered a presentation during the launch of the iPad. Please do watch it: **https://www.youtube.com/watch?v=QUuFbrjvTGw**. *Jobs* announced that when they designed the iPad to make it customer friendly, there was a lot of debate on a lot about profits, prices, investment, and all that, however they were about to conclude on the price- $999. Please refer to the following figure:

Figure 15.8: Steve Jobs launching iPad

They however, reevaluated this and discussed how they could make it more affordable while making sure that they did justice to the price and the product. So we decided to launch it at only $499. And then the crowd welcomed this price with heavy applause, a whistle, and a lot of joy.

This is a classy example of anchoring bias. Since he announced the price of $999 for the very first time, and when he announced it at $499, no one thought it was costly because he set it in everyone's mind that it is $500 cheaper than what it could have been. So ultimately, you are saving $500 when you buy this iPad.

This is such a classy example of anchoring bias. The way he presented the price, you got fixated on only the information that this iPad is $500 cheaper. Here, price **is** the anchor, because customers do not want to know about the performance or other aspects. The price becomes the main anchor for making the decision to buy an iPad. And of course, there always is trust in Apple products.

Anchoring bias in UX design

In the realm of user experience, the anchoring bias can greatly influence user interactions with products and services. A positive initial experience can lead users to ignore potential defects or shortcomings. Conversely, a negative first impression might prompt users to give up on a product too soon. Designers should strive to develop a comprehensive user experience by exploring different solutions and considering diverse user viewpoints.

Although typically viewed as a cognitive shortcoming, anchoring bias can be strategically utilized by designers to steer users towards favorable results. By designing an initial experience that is captivating and engaging, designers set an anchor that guides users along a specific path or towards desired behaviors and goals. This approach is especially effective in onboarding sequences and in shaping perceptions of a brand.

Here are a few examples where anchoring bias impacts the UX design:

- **First impressions in visual design**: The initial visual presentation of a product can have a lasting impact on the user's perception of both the brand and the product's quality.

- **Impact of initial product recommendations**: The first item presented in a recommendation list can affect the user's opinion of the quality of the remaining items.

- **Pricing perception**: The initial price a user encounters sets a standard in their mind, shaping their views on what is considered expensive or affordable, thus influencing their buying choices.

- **Negotiation framework**: In negotiation settings, the initial offer establishes a baseline that influences all subsequent offers and counterproposals.

- **Influence of form defaults**: Pre-set values in forms can guide user responses.

- **Search result bias**: The foremost search result can alter the user's view of the relevance of subsequent results.

- **Shaping perceptions through onboarding**: The first experience a user has during onboarding can determine their overall impression of the product.

- **Survey response influence**: The sequence of questions in a survey can affect the responses given by users.

Tips to overcome anchoring biases

In the realm of UX design, it is important to be aware of the user's anchoring bias and here are few tips to tackle those:

- **Work on first impression**: I think the most important part is to take care of your user onboarding, because first impression is the last impression. Once the user builds an impression about your brand and product, that impression stay for a long time. So as UX professionals, it is most important to plan the onboarding journey of the user, which should be hassle free, smooth, and satisfying.

- **Research / user testing / gorilla testing**: Since you are solving the problem of the user, it is quite important to take the opinion of the real user on your final design and take feedback during the development phase as well. You may choose any of the routes; you may go full-fledged with usability testing or you may do as minimal as gorilla testing, As I have been emphasizing earlier as well, some research is better than no research.

- **Provide multiple perspectives**: Provide multiple perspectives of the information you share in your product so that it is more trustworthy, and users are not fixated on one kind of information for the product.

Anchoring bias is a potent cognitive influence that greatly shapes users' choices and perceptions in the field of UX design. Although it presents challenges, understanding its impact enables designers to develop more impactful and user-focused experiences. Employing a variety of research techniques and offering users diverse viewpoints helps designers lessen the effects of anchoring bias, leading to the creation of products that genuinely cater to user requirements.

I hope you have a good understanding of anchoring bias now and will be able to recognize your user's anchoring bias while adapting to a change. It is very important to be aware of the anchoring bias of the users while designing the layout and information for them.

With this chapter, we are done with all the important biases that I wanted to talk about briefly, but that is not all; there are a few more biases that I would urge you to study.

Conclusion

Now, not only this chapter, but it is time to recap what we have discussed in the book so far. We discussed multiple types of psychological theories and laws, psychological effects, and a few types of gamification and biases. Also, we discussed how it impacts the design and the user's behavior. I hope you can understand the value of psychology in design and the depth and fundamental knowledge that psychology brings to design.

With this, we come to the end of this book. I hope you enjoyed reading this book and will also be able to use these theories in your real life and upcoming projects of design. I am hopeful it will help you emerge as a great designer and a thoughtful leader.

Join our book's Discord space

Join the book's Discord Workspace for Latest updates, Offers, Tech happenings around the world, New Release and Sessions with the Authors:

https://discord.bpbonline.com

Index

R

real-life examples, Tesler's law 49
  Adobe Photoshop 53, 54
  DSLR camera 51, 52
  flyovers and bridges 50, 51
  traffic lights 50
Reciprocation 161
  examples 165-168
  exploring 163-165
  history 162, 163
  origin 162, 163
  social psychology roots 162
  takeaways 168
reinforcement 169
  history 169
  negative reinforcement 175-178
  origin 169, 170
  partial reinforcement 178, 179
  positive reinforcement 170-174
  takeaways 180, 181
research bias 199
  analysis bias 202
  history 199, 200
  selection/sampling bias 201
  types 201
Reverse Halo effect 106

S

scarcity principle 145
  history 145-152
  origin 145-151
  takeaways 152
Search Engine Optimization (SEO) 162
shared commitment 181
  history 181-186
  origin 181-186
Significant Objects project 94
social proof 153
  customer testimonials and user feedback
    154-160
  history 153, 154

  origin 153, 154
  takeaways 160, 161
status quo bias 203
Storytelling effect 91
  history 92-96
  usage tips 96-100

T

Tesler's law 47
  history 48, 49
  real-life examples 49, 50
  usage tips 55

V

Von Restorff effect 133
  examples 137
  history 134-136
  using, by UX designers 137, 138

Z

Zeigarnik effect 81
  history 82-86
  tips 89
  use cases 87-89

Made in the USA
Monee, IL
07 July 2026